W9-AYW-564

MAGNIFICENCE
AND
MISERY

MAGNIFICENCE AND MISERY

A Firsthand Account of
the 1897 Klondike Gold Rush

by E. HAZARD WELLS
edited by Randall M. Dodd

Doubleday & Company, Inc.
Garden City, New York
1984

Library of Congress Cataloging in Publication Data

Wells, E. Hazard.
Magnificence and misery.

Includes index.
1. Klondike River Valley (Yukon)—Gold discoveries.
2. Klondike River Valley (Yukon)—Description and
travel.   3. Wells, E. Hazard.   I. Dodd, Randall M.,
1954–   . II. Title.
F1095.K5W44   1984   917.19'1

ISBN: 0-385-18458-1
Library of Congress Catalog Card Number: 83-11637
Copyright © 1984 by Randall M. Dodd

To my wife, Patti,

for her love and support

Well may it be said that
magnificence and misery go
hand in hand on the Klondike.

E. Hazard Wells
November 12, 1897

CONTENTS

CONTENTS

INTRODUCTION

This book is an eyewitness account of the 1897 Klondike Gold Rush as reported and photographed by E. Hazard Wells for the Scripps-McCrae newspaper chain of 1897–98. The 1897 journey was the third and last time Wells traveled to Alaska as a newspaper reporter. The contacts and experience he gained on those three trips served him well in later life. E. Hazard Wells became a prominent citizen of Seattle, Washington, founding and publishing the Seattle *Star* and the original Seattle *Sun* (and others), as well as founding and presiding over a variety of successful business enterprises. It was his celebrity status as an Alaskan explorer that made Wells and his family instant members-for-life of the Seattle social elite of that time. And it is the combination of that fame and Wells's decision to live in Seattle which, eighty-odd years hence, makes possible the writing of this book.

The series of circumstances which culminated in the writing of *Magnificence and Misery* is as much a part of the story as the much earlier journeys of E. H. Wells; however, in telling them, I find myself in the somewhat undesirable position of giving the ultimate ending of this story away in the introduction to the book. Fortunately, since this work is not primarily biographical in focus, the tale of how it came to be written does not spoil the reading of Wells's eyewitness accounts of the Klondike Gold Rush.

After returning from Alaska in 1898, Wells spent the first couple of years touring and lecturing on the gold fields and life on the Klondike. Subsequently, about 1900, he decided to make his home in Seattle, so he packed up his wife, Annie, and his nine-year-old daughter, Maude, and moved into a residence on Seattle's fashionable Queen Anne Hill. Shortly thereafter, Wells founded and began publishing the highly successful Seattle *Star*. Mr. and Mrs. Edmond Hazard Wells were the toast of the town, and their rapid acceptance among the social elite virtually guaranteed that daughter Maude would marry a like-connected young gentleman. On November 28, 1911, at the age of twenty, Maude did just that when she married Harry B. Lear, son of a very prominent and wealthy Seattle family with extensive banking interests. The newlyweds were off on a one-month Hawaiian honeymoon, and one of the most important steps in the story of this book, the union of Maude Wells and Harry Lear, had been taken.

In 1918, the young Mr. and Mrs. Lear were on a vacation tour of Europe. As they were traveling through England, they spotted an old Tudor castle with which they were both instantly smitten. After some thought, they decided to have a replica of it built in Seattle. So Harry Lear obtained copies of the original sixteenth-century plans, had them updated and changed to suit "modern" building codes and conveniences, and then had the American version of Shoreham House built on a lot he purchased in the Webster Point area of Seattle. Shoreham is a perfect duplicate of the original in England, with the exception of being wired for electricity and having indoor plumbing and a central heating system, which was originally a coal-fired furnace but was changed to an oil burner when automatic furnaces became available. To make it as close a copy of its European counterpart as possible, the Lears had the brick of which it was built and the slate for the roof imported from England, the tile for the patios from Italy, all of the rosewood and oak paneling and decorative woodwork hand-carved and imported from literally all around the world—even the plumbing in Shoreham is solid brass throughout. The Lears moved into their new dwelling (which took nearly four years to construct) in 1924.

Meanwhile, Maude Wells Lear's father, E. H. Wells, was approaching his twilight years and, after making his fortune from a variety of endeavors, decided to live out his time in a somewhat warmer clime than that in Seattle. In the 1930s, Wells moved to southern California, where he lived until succumbing to a stroke in 1940 at the age of eighty. In the last several years before his death Wells had begun collecting material to write his autobiography. Unfortunately, he died before he got down to the actual writing, so all that remained was the material he had collected in an old wooden crate—several books filled with virtually all of the newspaper articles he had written during his career, his handwritten ledger/journal/diary from the 1897 trip, a book of his original photographs from that same trip, as well as several books full of memorabilia.

When Maude Wells Lear returned from her father's funeral, she brought that collection of material with her. Apparently for lack of a better place, she stored the box in the abandoned coal bin at Shoreham House, putting it there shortly after her father's death in 1940.

For most of the next thirty years, the books sat in their dark, dry hiding place completely unmolested. Maude Wells Lear died in the late 1940s. Her husband, Harry Lear, remarried in the 1950s, then died in the mid-1960s. After Harry Lear died, his widow moved out of Shoreham House (leaving the books behind), and the bank handling the estate put it up for sale. Even in good economic times, the demand for a forty-two-room house with almost 10,000 square feet of floor space is minimal, so Shoreham stood empty and unsold for over two years. During that time, everything of value that wasn't nailed down (and a lot of things that were) was taken out of the house—except, fortunately, that box of books in the coal bin, which was actually a small room off the "wood room," where the fuel for the house's five fireplaces was kept. Apparently, due to inaccessibility or lack of interest, that one box was overlooked.

Eventually one of the potential buyers contacted my father, a structural engineer, and asked him to inspect the house, which had settled somewhat and taken a tilt toward Lake Washington, though so slight as to be noticeable only in certain areas inside the house. My father's client had no interest in the house whatsoever—he merely wanted to develop the two waterfront lots between Shoreham House and the water by subdividing the estate.

Coincidentally, at that time my family had outgrown its original home and was considering relocation to more spacious quarters. My father recognized the potential in Shoreham House almost immediately, and brought the plans home, where we held an impromptu family meeting. My brother, sister, mother and I all cast votes in favor of moving to Shoreham. After some wrangling over details, we ended up with Shoreham, *sans* subdivision, and moved in in April 1968.

While leading a flashlight expedition into the lower levels of the house shortly after we moved in, I stumbled (literally) across the box with Wells's work in it. I took it from its hiding place and showed the books to the rest of my family. We were all impressed by them, but didn't really read all of the material and so didn't realize the significance of the information it contained. Eventually my brother, sister and I all left home and my parents sold Shoreham House, but they took the books with them to their new home when they moved. On my part, I guess I always had that box of books somewhere in my mind, but it was to take nearly fifteen years before I remembered it and realized just how important a story it told.

During that time, I completed my college education and embarked on a career as a journalist. That particular choice of vocation led me to several years of frequent relocation, eventually landing me at a television station in Anchorage, Alaska, as a public affairs director and host of my own half-hour weekly show, as well as a news reporter and anchor. As such, I traveled to every corner of the state, meeting and talking with Alaskans from Juneau to Barrow, Nome to Fort Yukon. One of the things which struck me most in my travels around the state was how little most of the countryside has changed since the early days. I also developed a keen interest in the Gold Rush era of Alaskan history.

INTRODUCTION

That interest led me on a search for further information. During my research, I came across a list of the reporters who had covered the Gold Rush, one of which caught my attention. Try as I might, I could not remember where I had previously seen the name E. Hazard Wells. Eventually, it came to me—the memory was faint, but it seemed that E. H. Wells was the reporter who had written all of the material in the books I found in the coal bin more than a decade before.

After another delay of several months, I went back to Seattle on vacation. I dug out the box of books and read all of them cover-to-cover. My recollection proved accurate—Wells was indeed the author of all of the material. But what I hadn't remembered was how incredible an account of the early days of Alaska was contained in those pages.

When I finished reading and studying Wells's writings, I came to the conclusion that they were much too important to simply be thrown back into their dusty corner for another generation, and the book you are about to read is the offspring of that decision plus the myriad of circumstances and coincidences which made it possible.

I would like to extend thanks to the following: the University of Washington libraries, particularly the Northwest Collection, the Special Collections Department, and Dennis Anderson; the Instructional Media Services Department at the University of Washington and Stan Shockey for doing such a great job with the photographs; James Greiner; Chuck Morell; and my parents, Harvey and Velma Dodd, for making both the book and me possible.

Finally, since any book is a collaborative effort, I would like to extend special thanks to Louise Gault, my editor at Doubleday, and her assistant, Kathy Bayer, for all of the help they've been in the execution of this project, as well as to me personally as a new author.

FOREWORD

This story is told primarily from two sources. The first is the collection of all the newspaper articles Wells wrote during his 1897 Gold Rush trip. For the most part, those articles appear in their original form and are designated as follows: (for example) *Dawson City, N.W.T., October 10, 1897.*

The second source is Wells's handwritten ledger/journal/diary. A good portion of his handwritten diary is made up of transcriptions of his newspaper articles and, except where noted, these passages appear under their datelines as in the example in the previous paragraph. The journal entries which did not find their way into print are designated as follows: (for example) *August 13, 1897* (by date only, with location, if necessary, following in parentheses).

One further note of clarification: the dollar values given in the text regarding gold are all based on the 1897 price of $16 per ounce. The author wouldn't presume to predict what the price of gold will be by the time this book is published; however, as of this writing it is vacillating between $400 and $500 per ounce. For a quick and easy conversion of the gold values in this text to their approximate modern equivalents, simply multiply the number given in the text by 30.

FOREWORD

On July 26, 1897, Wells began his journey. His writings appeared in the Cincinnati *Post,* Cleveland *Press* and Covington *Kentucky Post,* which made up the Scripps-McRae syndicate of that time. On that Monday, the twenty-sixth, the Cincinnati *Post* ran the following article under the headline: OFF FOR THE KLONDIKE!!!

What is the truth about Klondike? Everybody is guessing. The *Post* will tell. The [Scripps-McRae syndicate] will have their own correspondent in the Klondike gold fields. He will be a man in whose competency and fidelity these papers have confidence. He will be a man in whose capabilities and truthfulness the *Post*'s readers, from old experience, will have confidence.

For this arduous service E. Hazard Wells has been chosen. It is the third time that Mr. Wells has been sent into Alaska to write up the scenery, topography and resources of that vast and wealthy portion of the great Northwest. Those who have read his letters on the two former trips will not need to be assured of the interest and practical worth of the correspondence expected from him from the Klondike fields.

Mr. Wells left Cincinnati today. He goes by way of Chicago, St. Paul, Seattle, Skagway, Lake Bennett, B.C., and on to Dawson.

Mr. Wells will begin an interesting series of letters at once, telling of the excitement about the Klondike discoveries as he goes from point to point on his great journey.

And so *Magnificence and Misery* begins—with Wells's first dispatch upon arriving in Chicago.

PART I

THE JOURNEY
TO KLONDIKE

Chicago, July 27, 1897

I arrived here on my journey to Klondike early Sunday morning, and I soon learned that the gold fever is raging in this city. It has become epidemic. Chicago is stirred from center to horizon by the agitation over Alaska gold. The silver question has been relegated to the background. Silver, in fact, seems no longer attractive except to the Pullman porters and hotel waiters.

The papers teem with vivid descriptions of the Yukon, largely imaginative, but nevertheless quite readable. One paper gravely describes the terrors of the region and forces the thermometer down to 90 degrees below zero. It is quite interesting to one who has been there and knows the milder truth.

But the Chicagoites are eager for gold, and many of them are going to Alaska. Hundreds have already started. I interviewed Colonel P. B. Weare, the well-known grain operator and Alaskan trader.

He operates a line of steamers from Seattle to the Yukon by way of Bering Sea and St. Michael and sells equipment and provisions to the miners.

"I'm afraid there's going to be trouble in the Klondike country soon," he remarked. "Both the Alaska Commercial Company and my own people have been laboring to get sufficient supplies up the Yukon to properly provision the trading posts for the coming winter. We have food enough in sight for 11,000 persons. There are at least 7000 in the Yukon Valley now, and other thousands are pouring into the country over the Chilkoot Pass and by way of St. Michael. There will probably be 11,000 or 12,000 there within the next two or three weeks.

"Now, what I fear is that a greater rush will take place as soon as our steamship, the *Portland,* arrives from St. Michael on August 20 with another cargo of gold. I don't know just how much is coming, but it is likely to be considerable.

"The country cannot well stand the strain of another shipload of gold right now. It is sure to set thousands of people crazy, and there is no telling what will happen. I greatly fear that a vast and uncontrollable multitude will rush up to Juneau all through September and October and invade the country in a mad quest for gold. There will be thousands without proper food and equipment, and they will plunge into the midst of the snow and terrors of an Arctic winter. What will the result be? With 30,000 or 40,000 persons on the Klondike, and food for but 11,000, there can be but one sequel.

"I would urge everyone who is thinking of going in by way of Chilkoot Pass to carry over enough provisions for his own use. As for the traders, we will continue to do our utmost. I have today wired to Seattle to have another provisions ship chartered at once and sent with a big cargo and no passengers direct to the Yukon. We have other steamers going that will carry both passengers and provisions."

"Have any quartz veins been located yet?" I asked.

"Yes, eight or nine, and assays will be made of the ore. Considerable quartz has been discovered, but it is well to attend to the placers for a while. There is gold enough in Alaska, and it is not all going to be taken out this year, or next year. It will keep, and I wish some of the people who are so eager to get into the country would just wait until next spring."

4

On Great Northern Train, Leaving St. Paul, July 28, 1897

"All aboard for Minneapolis, Seattle, and Klondike!" called out the Chicago depot master in stentorian tones.

Perhaps it was a joke, but it meant something serious to me, and I hustled for the train.

Away we sped through the dark night, with the cowcatcher pointed straight toward Klondike and with our anticipations racing madly ahead of the engine, leaping over rivers, lakes and mountain chains and sweeping across the British Northwest into the new El Dorado of the Yukon.

It was a glorious feeling, like that which comes to a fellow on the eve of his wedding, or when a millionaire maiden aunt takes passage for another sphere, leaving her baggage checks behind.

Into St. Paul we rolled, and found the town even more excited than Chicago.

"On to Klondike!" was the magic watchword.

The gun stores were busily retailing .45-90 Winchesters. The gum blanket men, who also sell rubber boots, were enjoying a rushing trade. The department stores were hoisting bales of camphorated woolens out of their cellars to supply the midsummer demand. It seemed queer, but "Klondike" explained it all.

With another Klondiker I made the rounds, picking up a Winchester here, gum boots there and heavy woolens just around the corner. A procession of porters was soon en route to the hotel with the outfit.

Said one merchant to me, "We had a Klondiker yesterday who was carrying a canvas canoe. He was sure that he could get across Chilkoot Pass and go skimming down the Yukon without a care. Said he knew all about the business."

Perhaps he does, but it's dollars to beans he'll know still more about it before he gets past the Grand Canyon of the Yukon.

Really, St. Paul is Klondikized to a remarkable extent. Every other man one meets is anxious to move northward, and many are starting on the journey. The newspapers are running Klondike departments and are adding to the excitement.

At the offices of the Great Northern Railway and of the Northern Pacific there are streams of callers, all asking information concerning Klondike, demanding rates and buying tickets.

Steamship berths are reserved at Seattle by telegraph, and the wires are kept hot at all times.

Every overland train carries from 10 to 30 gold seekers en route to Alaska and the Yukon Valley. Most of them purchase second-class, or tourist, one-way tickets. Nobody, in fact, thinks of getting a round-trip nine-month ticket. Who would be so foolish?

It looks as though the rush of men to Alaska is just beginning. The whole country is aroused over the Klondike discoveries. The nation has been seized with the disease of the wandering foot, one of the gravest complications resulting from the gold fever.

Some are going to Alaska who have money and provisions to stand the trip. They may do well. A multitude of poor fellows are, however, heading for the gold fields who will bitterly regret their adventure before many months have passed. With hardly money enough to pay their passage to Chilkoot, they are preparing to rush into the Yukon, depending upon only their wits to exist until spring. An Arctic winter will come roaring down the valley during the October moon. Without proper clothing and with no food or money to buy from the traders, they will be in a terrible plight. I know what the consequence will be. Thousands of corpses will lie on the mountainsides and in the valleys unless a good Providence shall actively intervene.

Out of the awful terrors of the coming winter, out of the destruction of human lives, will, however, be evolved the settlement and prosperity of Alaska. The complete exploration and speedy development of the Territory is assured.

With thousands of eager gold seekers in the Yukon Valley who can find no "claims," there is bound to result a scattering of the multitude far and wide throughout Alaska. Every river and creek, every mountain chain will be explored in the frantic search for the hidden gold. The mysterious Mount Wrangell country, with its great active volcano, will be penetrated, and the 1200 square miles of untrodden wilderness beyond will unlock its secrets, unknown today even to the fur traders.

Gold will be found in many new places. It is scattered in rich deposits throughout the Territory, and the searchers will find it. Then look out for renewed excitement in "the States."

It is the prediction of experienced mining men that next year the rush of gold seekers will be comparable to nothing except the California excitement of '49.

With the influx of people will come the development of new industries.

Salmon canneries upon the Yukon will be established for the first time. There are fish enough in the great river to keep a hundred canneries running for years. The experiment of wintering cattle in Alaska will be tried. There is plenty of grass.

Other avenues of enterprise will open up, and permanent towns will be established in the interior and on the seacoasts. Who dare say that Alaska, with its great resources in gold, copper and coal, and its possibilities in other directions, will not speedily become a prosperous and thickly populated portion of Uncle Sam's domain? For my part, I expect it.

Seattle, Washington, July 30, 1897

Seattle is wild over the report that $3,000,000 more of gold is on the way from Alaska.

Trains from the East and South are bringing hundreds of gold seekers to this place daily, and thousands more are reported to be en route. Alaska outfitting seems to be the sole business of this city at present. Shiploads of packhorses are being rushed to Chilkoot, where a blockade of 1000 men with freight is reported.

The packing rates from Chilkoot to the Yukon have risen from

As Wells states, the arrival of a "treasure ship" loaded with Alaskan gold was a major event in Seattle. Here, the steamer Roanoke *arrives from the north with $4 million in gold dust.*

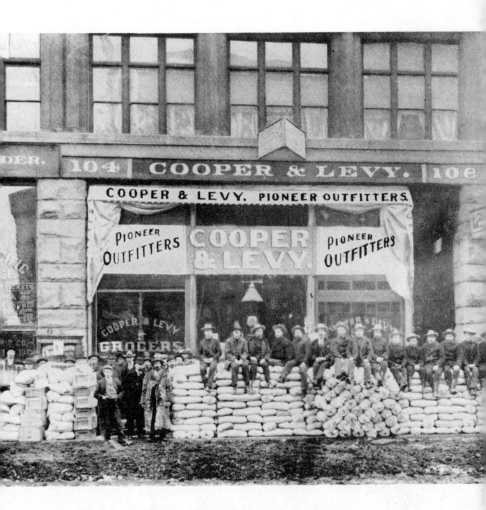

Typical Seattle Klondike outfitter of the Gold Rush era.

The cargo of the Roanoke.

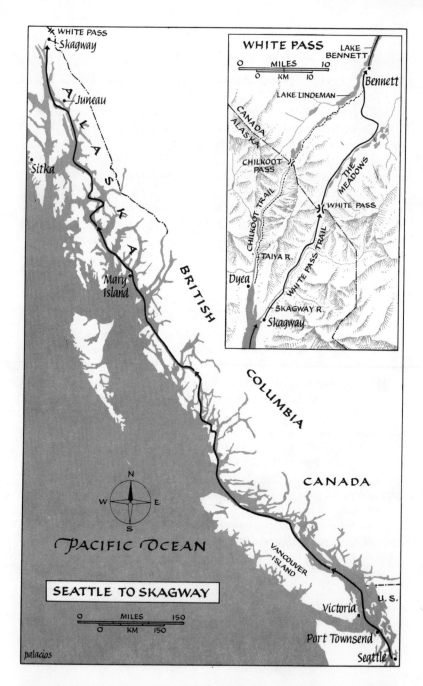

Map showing the route of the Rosalie *from Seattle to Skagway, Alaska. Inset shows the "White Pass Trail" from Skagway to Lake Bennett, B.C.*

15 to 22 cents per pound. Hundreds cannot get packhorses yet at any price.

Your correspondent's day in this gold-fever-stricken town was spent in securing final supplies for the "grubstake," as well as half interest in two packhorses for the journey over White Pass to the Yukon. The latter were secured from a grocery-wagon yard for the extorted price of $50, fully twice what such beasts might bring in less demanding times. They are hardy fellows of the draught type, however, and will surely be a valuable asset on the trail, having spent the first half of their existence pulling loaded grocery wagons up and down the steep hills of Seattle.

I sail tomorrow for Alaska aboard the steamer *Rosalie.*

Mary Island, Alaska, August 3, 1897

Our group of Klondikers left Seattle at 9:20 P.M. on the eve of Saturday, July 31. The horses were sent earlier that day aboard the steamship *Edith.*

Our first stop was on Sunday, August 1, at Port Townsend, Washington, where several more passengers boarded and mail was taken ashore. We have been traveling the Inland Passage to Alaska since that time.

The fogbound solitudes of the British Columbian coast from Vancouver to Alaska are re-echoing today with the hoarse shrieks of steamship whistles. Slipping like phantoms through the thick, white mist, appear and disappear the huge forms of the floating caravansaries which are bearing northward the eager army of gold seekers. The Chilkoot gates leading into the Ice King's domain have clearly been forced by the vanguard of the army, and a continuous stream of agitated humanity is pouring into the new El Dorado.

The somber reaches of the mighty Yukon, which have but seldom been trodden by the foot of white men, are now the scene of novel activities. In all directions are heard the thud of the pick and the scraping of the shovel. Log cabins are springing into view at

11

every river bend where the swirling of the waters has deposited gold-bearing sands. Companies of men are rushing hither and thither, drawn by the exciting reports of new placer discoveries.

Such are the rumors drifting down to those of us on the *Rosalie* as we are borne ever onward toward Alaska. Each passing southbound ship brings some item of late news from the gold fields, which is eagerly caught up and discussed. One rumor has it that the Chilkoot Pass, leading into the Yukon, is clogged and jammed by the mighty multitude which is struggling to get across. Carts, packhorses, dog trains and men are said to be mixed up in inextricable confusion. If this report is true, it portends great dangers.

Winter is already striding down from the Arctic, and the frozen mountains may engulf the host, even as the army of Pharaoh was engulfed in the Red Sea.

Few of the searchers for gold have any realization of the terrors of an Arctic winter, and the larger proportion have gone illy prepared for the emergencies which will surely confront them. The Angel of Death will stalk abroad in the Yukon next winter, reaping a harvest of frozen victims, unless all of the signs of the day shall prove untrue.

The *Rosalie,* on which I travel, is a small Puget Sound steamboat, which has been pressed into the Alaskan service for an indefinite period. It is loaded down to the guards with freight and passengers.

The list of people aboard, besides the crew, includes 140 men and three married women, one of whom, Mrs. A. T. French of Seattle, proposes to accompany her husband and brother across the mountains and into the gold regions. She is a pretty, vivacious lady, apparently under 36, and is attired in a natty blue velvet costume. She wears a dainty feather in her cap and red ribbons on her hair. Mrs. French evidently believes in "keeping up appearances" even on the rolling sea. Her husband is a little, smooth-shaved man of kindly, patient mien and wears a broad-brimmed desperado's hat that illy becomes his style and build.

Perhaps some of the men on board ship envy French because he has such a charming girl along with him.

She has a fascinating manner and an independent spirit that has captivated half of the men aboard, including some who have wives at home. Her influence, however, is for good. She is of religious disposition, and insists on having every broad-brimmed fellow in the ship sing from Gospel Hymns No. 6. Several tried to start "Annie Rooney" Sunday night, but she choked them off politely, not with her hands but with her Gospel Hymns. Mrs. French left her two children in Seattle with her parents. She decided that, as between Joseph and the children, the former more needed her wifely care and attention.

The other two women aboard are merely going to Juneau and have no intention of entering the interior of Alaska, at least this fall.

As for the men, they comprise all classes, except sharpers and gamblers. It is surprising, in fact, to notice the entire absence of the gambling element from among the passengers. Not one game of chance, with cards, has been played for money since the *Rosalie* left Seattle, although no restrictions of any kind are imposed upon the boat. The company of 140 men is largely composed of ex-merchants, clerks, farmers, laborers from the cities, with a sprinkling of street-car drivers, lawyers and photographers. There is a most remarkable and delightful esprit de corps prevailing.

Social combinations between the ex-merchants, the day laborers and the fashionable young men who formerly sold ribbons over the counter are all the "go." Nobody wears a "better than thou" frown above his necktie. Equality, good fellowship and hopefulness are the basic principles controlling this floating community. It is pleasant. It is ideal. At the "ladies' table," in the little dining room belowdecks, the men all respectfully take off their hats while eating dinner. At the other table most of the diners prefer to keep their headwear on, as there is no good place to hang hats up, except on the floor.

The meals served on board the *Rosalie* have not been prepared with an idea of pampering the passengers. In fact, there is an evident scheme running through the biscuits, meat and pastry to harden the stomachs of the people to a Yukon bill of fare. Only one man has complained to date, and his unpleasant adjectives concerning the biscuits were promptly silenced by a stern-looking Klondiker, who remarked, "If this fellow can't stand half-cooked grub now, what the devil will he do when he gets into the mountains, where they eat things raw?"

We have one mint-julep-and-oyster-stew man aboard. He is a young New Yorker, in black velveteen pantaloons, who vibrates between a whiskey bottle and a box of cigars like Galileo's pendulum. He is going to have his eyeteeth cut in Alaska. Next spring the chances are that this Eastern polka dot will be among the number who will return to the States with dismal stories concerning barren Alaska.

The *Rosalie* carries a varied and somewhat remarkable cargo. In addition to sacked provisions of all kinds, the miners have Klondike wagons, sleds, sectional boats and many other contrivances intended to lessen the time and labor usually consumed in getting to the mines. One man expects to load his 40-pound canvas canoe with 1400 pounds of outfit and go skimming away down the Yukon with no trouble to perplex. I warned him that rocky shoals lie all along the route and now he is uneasy.

The sectional boats lie stacked in piles upon the upper deck. Some are 16–24 feet in length, while others are not over 14 feet. All are built on a broad scale so as to permit the carrying of heavy cargoes.

It is noticeable that many of the miners who left Seattle arrayed in broad-brimmed hats and wearing big hobnailed shoes on their feet have already discarded these encumbrances for caps and tennis shoes. A number of them flopped about the decks for a day or two, like great auks, wearing their spiked footwear, until the officers of the ship objected to the dents left in the floors and woodwork. Then the Klondike shoes disappeared and a season of rubber-soled comfort was inaugurated.

Many of the men on board do not intend to go to Klondike, but will stop short 80 miles at Stewart River. It is believed that the

Klondike diggings are overrun with miners and that it is useless for more men to go there at present.

My own personal knowledge of Stewart River inclines to the belief that this stream is going to be the scene of some extensive gold-mining operations. It is a river as large as the Ohio and has many tributaries and gulches for 300 miles along its course. Fine flour gold can be had from any of the placer banks along the Stewart, and diggings have been profitably worked.

It yet remains for someone to locate coarse gold in the gulches along the Stewart, but there seems little doubt that this will be done during the next year. Stewart River is long enough to scatter 2000 miners along its basin without allowing them to feel at all crowded.

Pelly River, lying near the Stewart, and also a tributary of the Yukon, will be thoroughly explored, so will the Hootalinqua and a number of minor streams. There is plenty of room for everybody now in the country, and for thousands more to come. The only danger lies in the probable scarcity of provisions.

On the Steamer Rosalie, *Alaskan Waters, August 4, 1897*

Startling reports come from the Yukon Valley regarding the fate of several hundred men who are said to have recently perished in the Grand Canyon and Whitehorse Rapids while attempting to run through those places in boats.

The canyon is located on the Yukon, about 470 miles from headwaters, and terminates in the Whitehorse Rapids, which in turn end in falls, varying from 8 to 15 feet in height, according to the stage of the river. The bad water extends for three and one-half miles, and can be avoided only by portaging boat and outfit along the right-hand bank. This procedure involves a delay of several days, and the impatient gold seekers, in many instances, conclude to take chances, rather than lose time. So they point their boats' bows into the canyon and start on a wild race through the raging waters. The canyon is crooked and is seven-eighths of a mile in length. The swirl of the waters throws the daring adventurers from one side to the other and, perchance, dashes them against the rocky walls. In this case there is but little chance of escape. The boat is crushed, and occupants and cargo thrown into the river and lost.

Just below the canyon the Whitehorse Rapids begin, and if the boat survives the passage through the canyon the danger is aggravated in the seething water beyond. The Whitehorse is nothing more nor less than a great river tumbling downstairs. The roaring can be heard for several miles. The waters angrily splash and foam, throwing clouds of spray high into the air. The very atmosphere breathes of danger, and woe to the foolhardy men who brave its terrors in a small boat. A few have attempted the passage and have gone down safely, but the majority who have tried it have paid for their temerity with their lives.

It seems strange that men who have spent many weeks in toil and hardships, getting their outfits over the mountains, and have successfully faced all difficulties and dangers on their way down the Yukon to the canyon, should then deliberately stake their lives on an attempt to do a foolhardy and unnecessary thing; but such has been the sad history of more than one mining party. The gold hunger, the eager desire to get to the diggings as quickly as possible, seems to take over the cool judgment, the common sense of some men. I write these words of warning for the benefit of the multitude who expect to enter the Yukon country in the spring.

It is hard to trace the stories of those who have perished in the canyon this summer to an authentic source, owing to the distance they have traveled, but there can be no doubt that some imprudent Klondikers have perished in the angry waters. The place has been the scene of many fatalities in the past and will entrap more to their death in the years to come.

There are a few other dangerous places on the great river, but the canyon and the Whitehorse are by far the worst of all.

THE JOURNEY TO KLONDIKE

Many Eastern newspapers have recently been publishing absurd matter relating to the Klondike and the Alaskan gold fields, and these sheets are beginning to find their way up along the Alaskan coast and are causing considerable merriment, as well as annoyance. The New York *Journal* seems to be taking the lead in this faking business. I have just been shown a copy of the *Journal* of July 25 containing a Klondike page. The paper announced in an official tone of voice that Klondikers next spring will find the exact expense of a journey to the Yukon to foot up $1300, of which $500 must be expended for an Arctic dog team and sled and the balance for provisions, etc., for one year.

The truth of the matter is that Alaskan seacoast dogs cost on an average $3 to $5 apiece, and are never held in Juneau at a higher price than $10 each. A team consists of seven dogs, which, at the outside, will cost $70, while the sled is worth $10 or $12 more, making a total of $82 for the outfit, instead of $500. The *Journal*'s estimate of the cost of provisions and equipment is $600, whereas one year's provisions and outfit can be readily purchased in Seattle for $400, and on a very complete scale. Any man having $600 can leave New York or Cincinnati and reach the Klondike with a good outfit and a year's provisions.

I call attention to these errors merely because such misstatements are copied and spread broadcast through the land.

There are several Pacific Coast fakers already at work on Alaskan stories, and their numbers and audacity will doubtless increase as the winter months draw on and communication with the interior grows difficult. Several of these fakers are located comfortably at Seattle and Juneau, and from these points of vantage on the seacoast, they are dipping their pens in blood and sending out "eyewitness" accounts of starvation scenes on the Yukon.

The readers of this account will get the exact truth concerning the situation in the Yukon next winter, as I will be on the ground and will report conditions as they exist. It is no part of my program to invent fictitious scenes and events, but simply to tell the truth as I see it.

I fully expect that trouble will arise there because of the shortage of provisions. Too many people are already in the Yukon Valley to be supported on the supplies available at the trading posts. Many are in danger of starvation. The facts will not, however, be secured by the writers located in Seattle and Juneau, but by the very few newspapermen who will actually be on the ground.

It seems advisable at this time to warn all readers of these lines who contemplate a visit to the Alaskan gold fields and the Klondike country to postpone their adventure until next spring and then bring in their own provisions.

On Steamboat Rosalie, *Approaching Skagway, Alaska, August 6, 1897*

This is the last day of the voyage on salt water for our company of Alaska gold hunters.

Skagway, at the foot of White Pass, will be reached at 6 A.M. tomorrow and the passengers and cargo put ashore. No hotel runners will seize our grips. No omnibuses will stand lined up along the wharf. No "Grand Hotel" will receive us for breakfast. Skagway is not a town, but simply a spot of wet, mossy earth at the foot of a high mountain on the seashore. The only shelter from wind and rain is to be found in tents. Each passenger must look out for himself and his outfit. If it shall be raining in the morning he will put on his mackintosh and gum boots and stand by on the wharf to receive and protect his goods as best he can. There can be no delay in unloading the cargo, as the *Rosalie* must hurry back to Seattle to receive more gold hunters for Alaska.

There is considerable discussion among the passengers tonight as to where breakfast will come from on the morrow. It is the present understanding, however, that the captain will furnish the extra meal on board ship and that the passengers will then turn to and help unload the boat. Lawyers, clerks, merchants and farmers will all act as stevedores and hustle the stuff ashore. Each man is anx-

Wells's photograph of an earlier (identity unknown), less fortunate Gold Rush steamer. This view was taken from on board the Rosalie *en route to Skagway.*

Another view of the Inland Passage to Alaska, as photographed by Wells from the deck of the Rosalie.

Another Wells photograph from the Rosalie, *notable chiefly for its moving subject. Owing to the extremely slow speed of the film at the time, this "live action" type of photograph was extremely difficult to achieve.*

ious to get hold of his own belongings and to get started on the Yukon trail.

The breakfast will have the summer luxury of ice water, and the ice will be Alaskan. Ice, which started a hundred years ago or more from some Alaskan ravine, away up the mountainside, and which has been traveling seaward ever since, forming part of a slowly but ceaselessly moving glacier, now floats in great fragments about the *Rosalie.* Two of these miniature bergs were hoisted aboard ship today, and will stock the ice room of the *Rosalie* on the return voyage.

(Photographed for The Post by E. Hazard Wells.)

UPPER DECK OF THE ROSALIE, SHOWING SECTIONAL BOATS PILED UP.

Sketched from a Wells photo, this drawing shows how some of Wells's fellow passengers on the Rosalie *looked.*

As the steamer approaches Skagway the excitement among the passengers visibly increases. It has been a noisy, cheering, enthusiastic crowd from the start, and the symptoms of gold delirium are growing more and more pronounced.

A dozen men are standing about on the deck with rifles and revolvers, banging away at icebergs, seals, gulls and porpoises with a reckless disregard of the cost of ammunition. It is not against the rules of the ship to pop away at any hour of the day or night, but the captain has cautioned the rifle users to be prudent and shoot none of the other passengers. Up to the present time this advice has been accepted.

The waters of the passage or sound up which we are steaming are alive with small craft of every description, all heavily laden with miners' outfits and supplies and heading toward Skagway.

Afar in the rear the black smoke of a steamship is seen spreading out over the horizon. "It is another gold hunters' ship coming up behind," remarked the captain, "but she will not overhaul us before we reach Skagway."

Yesterday the *George W. Elder* passed us crowded with miners and laden with supplies. Not a day goes by but what one, two or three steamboats discharge hundreds of passengers and their outfits at Skagway.

The magnificent scenery along the Inland Passage from Seattle to Skagway has attracted little attention from the majority of our ship's company. The restless anxiety to get to Alaska and rush across the mountains to the Yukon has dominated every other feeling and impulse. The cabin is continually crowded with men who are discussing dried fruits and vegetables, evaporated vinegar, packhorses and mining laws.

Occasionally some fellow looks out of the cabin door at the gloomy, fog-wrapped mountains guarding the Alaska coast, and shivers as a cold glacial blast comes over the sea and penetrates his personality. With a shrug he closes the door and returns to the crowd engaged in the interminable debates on the virtues of desiccated vegetables.

22

My personal knowledge of the interior of Alaska has caused me to be the target for thousands of questions concerning the country, the trail, etc., all of which I have endeavored to answer with patience and precision.

Half the ship's company had already heard of me as the original discoverer of the Klondike, and there is a large number who want to go into Alaska with me. The idea seems to have got abroad that I know where all the gold is located and am a sort of second Moses who can lead these children of Mammon into the Promised Land.

Skagway, Alaska, August 7, 1897

Our brave band of Klondikers reached this location late in the afternoon of yesterday. We found an enormous concourse of people camped on the beach and in the woods.

The *Rosalie* tied up to a partly finished wharf of the Skagway Trading and Transportation Company. Every Klondiker was required to pay one dollar wharfage and then get his goods moved as quickly as possible. The wharf, however, was built against a cliff, so that it was impracticable, at times impossible, to carry stuff ashore except in boats, for which extravagant prices were asked. A boat- or skiff-load cost from $2 to $3 each, and the distance to be traversed from ship to shore was less than 200 yards. Goods were dumped at low tide or high tide, just as it happened, and owners had to rustle to move things back from the encroachments of the sea. Eugene Grever, my traveling companion and owner of the other half of our two-horse pack "team," and I camped about one-half mile back from the salt water. Our two horses had been successfully jumped from the landing scow, and were allowed to roam on open grassland and feed overnight.

Wells took this photograph from the bow of the Rosalie *as it arrived at Skagway, Alaska, on the morning of August 7, 1897.*

Skagway, Alaska, August 10, 1897

One of the most thrilling scenes of modern times is being enacted at this point. A vast army of men, brawny and muscular, are engaged in a desperate attempt to blast and cut the White Trail through the Chilkat Mountains to the Yukon River. The mountainsides and gulches are resounding to the ring of a thousand axes felling the great trees along the chosen route, while hundreds of pounds of dynamite and giant powder are being hastily prepared for transportation to points in the mountains where blasting will be necessary. Tomorrow it is intended to put 800 men at work bridging chasms and cutting a path along Sentinel Butte, the first serious obstacle in the way of the invading host of Klondikers.

24

Semi-military law has been established in the Skagway camp; with no semblance of civil authority in this city of tents, it became absolutely necessary to at once form a provisional government for mutual protection. This movement took form at a mass meeting of miners held yesterday at 2 P.M., at which a veteran from Montana named Dave McKinney was chosen chairman. He in turn appointed a vigilance committee of thirty men to execute the will of the camp, as expressed by popular voice. The first job in hand was attending to the case of Job Cleveland, a teamster, who was accused of charging $10 for the cartage of a dead man's body from Skagway River to the camp. This unfeeling act aroused such a tempest of indignation that Cleveland had a narrow escape from being lynched. He was ordered to leave camp by 10 A.M. today or suffer the consequences. He fled precipitately.

The difficulty arose as the result of the drowning of Dwight Fowler, aged 23, of Seattle. Dwight was attempting to cross the wide mountain torrent called the Skagway River at a point only three-quarters of a mile from the camp. It was the regular crossing point, a slippery log over which the water foamed being the only foothold. He carried a pack on his back. Missing his footing, he fell headlong into the raging flood and in a twinkling disappeared from view. Half a dozen men, including myself, who were eyewitnesses of the occurrence, endeavored in vain to assist him. He rose to the surface fully 200 feet below the point where he first sank, his pack buoying him up, and rolled over and over in the tumbling waters, his face gashed and bleeding from cuts received in striking snags and trees. It was a horrible sight!

Several hundred yards farther down the stream, where it narrowed between two sandbanks, a young man, a partner of Fowler's, rushed out into the flood and seized the body as it approached. By this time life was extinct. The remains were solemnly carried ashore and then many of the men resumed their work of packing across the slippery log.

In the meanwhile, teamster Cleveland, who owned one of the few wagons in camp, came by and carried the corpse half a mile to the tent of Will Fuller, leader of Fowler's party, demanding $10 for his services. The men standing about were astounded at the demand and offered a remonstrance, which was received with an oath and another demand for the money. Finally, one of the boys went down into the dead man's pocket, took out a wet roll of money and, selecting a $10 bill, handed it to the fellow. The news of the affair spread with lightning-like rapidity and an ominous muttering was heard, which reached Cleveland's ears. He offered to return the money, but it was refused. Then the formal meeting was held which drummed him out of camp.

The death of Fowler and the narrow escape of several other men from a similar fate in the river resulted in an impromptu movement to build a bridge. This was carried on with vigor, and within 86 hours the 100-man crew had a heavy log-pier corduroy bridge in four spans thrown across the stream. It will be formally opened tomorrow. In the meantime, news came from the front that the trail was not opened through to the Yukon over a practicable route and that it was almost impassable for men or horses. The half a hundred men who had forced their way to the first summit sent back word that blasting for one-fourth of a mile would be necessary in order to straighten the trail and avoid passing over a high and precipitous mountain.

Again a meeting was called, for eleven o'clock this morning, and a large crowd responded. Chairman McKinney presided on a stump, and your correspondent, as the only man in the crowd who had even been in the Yukon country, was called upon for a speech. I took McKinney's place on the stump and made the worst effort of my life. I cautioned the miners against allowing men to cross to the Yukon without sufficient food to last them through the eight months' winter, and quoted my own grisly experience with starvation in Alaska in 1890 while exploring the interior.[1] I warned them that unless the movement to leave without enough provisions should be checked by summary measures, fully half of them

[1]Wells is referring to his reporting trip for *Frank Leslie's Illustrated Newspaper;* at one point in the journey he and his companions were forced to eat their dog.

Wells took this photograph of Klondikers on the beach at Skagway shortly after his arrival.

would perish before next May. The greed for gold which was causing many men to drop their provisions and rush ahead of their fellows toward the Yukon was, as I expressed it, a crime scarcely short of downright murder, as these men would become like wolves, preying upon the men who had something to eat.

There will be a fight to the death and terrible times unless things are properly conducted now. The trail must be properly cut through and men compelled to carry at least 700 pounds of provisions apiece, or sent back to the seacoast. I further quoted Yukon trader Weare's statement, made to me in Chicago, that there were insufficient supplies at the Yukon trading posts to support the incoming multitude.

27

The speech, wretched as it was in style and rhetoric, produced the desired effect. Nobody wanted to starve. Action was taken immediately. A committee of ten men, including myself, was appointed to go at once over the trail to the difficult place and decide upon a plan for operations. The committee was further given despotic authority to compel all men in the camp to do their share of the trail cutting or run them out of camp.

Tonight we go up seven miles to the mountain, where the blasting is reported to be necessary, and will return to camp by morning to promulgate a plan of procedure. We propose to put the trail through at any cost and to reach the Yukon this fall.

Skagway, Alaska, August 12, 1897

A wild stampede into the mountains is in progress and all semblance of method and order has been lost. It is a case of every man for himself, with Old Nick bringing up the rear.

The miners' mass meeting a few days ago resulted in the collection of a considerable sum of money for blasting a trail. A large body of men, perhaps 175 in number, under the command of the provisional executive committee, including your correspondent, started into the mountains to rebuild the old trail, but the gold hunger grew so keen that after a few corduroy bridges had been thrown across marshes and streams the attempt was abandoned and a general helter-skelter ensued.

The trail over White Pass is jammed with horses, goods and men, and catastrophes are occurring every hour. This morning it is reported that over twenty pack animals·have pitched off of bad places along the mountainsides. One entire packtrain was thrown, but the animals were all recovered. Every day a number are maimed or killed. The jam of horses going and returning along the trail is so great that many altercations ensue between the drivers over the right-of-way, and bloodshed is daily expected.

Enough provisions to load a large ocean steamer have been started up the mountains and are stranded all along the way. Not one-tenth of the stuff can ever be portaged across the Yukon.

The few packtrains are worked to death and their owners are demanding and receiving fabulous prices for their services. No packer now thinks of asking less than $1500 for portaging 1500 pounds of outfit across the divide. In other words, packing rates have about reached the dollar-per-pound level. Even at this price there is an overwhelming demand.

Men seem to have gone stark crazy at the prospect of being foiled in their attempts to cross the mountains and are willing to pay any price or do anything in order to carry their point. Fully 2000 Klondikers with their 2000 outfits are struggling along the beginning of the trail. None of them want to turn back and go home to face their friends. Most prefer to winter in the mountains along the route regardless of consequences. Men with haggard faces, unkempt hair and disordered attire are seen plodding along groaning under the weight of 100-pound packs. Perspiration is bursting from every pore in their bodies and their breaths come hard and fast.

"Great Scott, but we are earning our grubstakes!" exclaimed one fellow as he staggered past. Men who a few short weeks ago were holding easy clerical positions are now slaving like longshoremen to get their grub advanced a few paces along the trail leading into the new El Dorado. I have noticed a number of sporting women in several of the parties, but there is a woeful scarcity of ladies. Only one, Mrs. French, of Seattle, has so far attempted the trail.

A packer who returned from the Yukon end of the trail yesterday told me that only ten men with their provisions had yet succeeded in getting across the mountains, although others of the vanguard were appearing near at hand. At Lake Bennett, where the trail ends, a small sawmill is reported to be in operation, where a dozen men are busy at work at $10 a day cutting up timber for boats. The retail price of these watercraft, which are of the crudest possible construction, varies from $75 to $150 apiece, according to size. Timber is scarce along the lake, and the mill owner gets his supply by bargaining with miners to cut logs and bring them to the mill, the miners getting one-fourth of their logs cut up free of charge. The mill owner gets the other three-fourths of the logs without a cent of expense.

High prices for horses rule all along the trail from Skagway to the Yukon. No offer of less than $175 per animal is ever considered.

Two days ago a horseless Klondiker met me on the trail and the following dialogue ensued:

STRANGER: Have you got any horses for sale?

CORRESPONDENT: No, I have two, but I need them.

STRANGER: I'll give you $175 each.

CORRESPONDENT: No.

STRANGER: Look here, man, I've got to get in, even if your horses cost me $300 each.

EXCITED CORRESPONDENT: You don't get them for $300 each or any other sum. I've got to reach the Yukon whether you do or not!

AMAZED STRANGER: Well, I'll be goshed!

A fortune could have been made by any man who would have brought a cargo of horses to Skagway in August. By September there will be horses to give away, and to shoot. The word has gone south that horses are needed, and thousands are reported to be on the way.

The glut in provisions along the trail makes stuff absolutely unsalable. Bacon and flour cannot be given away. If you offer a sack to a man he politely refuses it and asks you to visit his tent and take some away. Nobody knows what to do with all of his plunder. Men who expect to reach the Yukon this fall by way of the so-called White Pass must sacrifice most of their outfits. Attempts to portage any considerable amount of goods are certain to fail.

The most discouraging news today is to the effect that Billy Ames, one of the few packtrain owners on the trail, has announced that he cannot fill more than three or four of his contracts to pack across the range, as his horses will succumb to the terrible ordeal. He is canceling contracts worth thousands of dollars.

White Pass, in its present inaccessible shape, is a trap, and should be avoided unless put into proper shape before next spring. An attempt is to be made today to found this town of Skagway, on the oceanfront; and then, if the project shall succeed, a public subscription will be raised to blast and cut a good trail through to the Yukon. Town lots are already for sale on the beach, at prices varying from $3.50 to $50, although there has been no government or private survey, and nobody knows where the "lots" begin or end. There are two wooden buildings in Skagway and half a hundred tents. Provisions have no fixed price, but tinware cannot be bought at any price. There is none in "town."

There is absolute certainty that five-sixths of the people now struggling to get over White Pass will be foiled by the winter, which is due here within six weeks, and these will either have to build cabins along the trail and winter in the mountains, or be thrown back into Skagway. My prediction is that the town will have fully 3000 population during the coming cold season, and perhaps there will be twice as many more. As Skagway has no industries of any kind to support it, I fail to see what the people will do to earn a living, except to speculate off of the newcomers from "the States."

This morning I met a gentleman from New York. We will call him Jones. He told me that he had once been wealthy, but had failed in business and owed a large sum of money to his creditors. He had for several years been trying to repay them out of the savings of his salary as a bookkeeper, but finding that it would take too many years, he had thrown up his position and had determined to risk all in the Yukon. "My hair is gray," he remarked, "and my time is short. I must succeed in Alaska, so as to clear myself of debt

31

before I die." The man was honest in appearance and seemed desperately determined.

The newspaper world is not as well represented at Skagway as I had expected to find it. The New York *World* threw its banner to the breeze in Skagway today, with Sylvester Scovill as correspondent, but, outside of myself, there are no other bona fide newspapermen in the vicinity. Several miners have told me that they are to send news to various papers, but there is little journalistic work being done. Everyone is too busy looking after himself in the general rush to get over the trail.

It is a noticeable fact that the Klondikers are mostly green men in the mountains and find camp life a new experience. The "bread" that is baked in some camps would kill a mule. "Oh, for a loaf of Mother's bread!" is the wail that is heard on every hand. The heavy Klondike shoes, bristling with spikes and armor plate, which the Seattle dealers sold to the boys as "the only thing for the mountains," are being generally cast aside. Every man I meet envies me my lightweight tennis shoes, and I could sell a thousand at $5 per pair if I had a stock on hand. "That man Wells has been in the Yukon twice" is the remark that I hear twenty times a day, and then some tenderfoot stops me for advice.

I am the only man on the trail who has ever seen the Yukon, and I have been obliged to wear the aspect of a wiseacre and give much paternal advice to men old enough to be my grandfather. It is flattering to be so well known in a mining camp, but the accompanying responsibilities are somewhat unpleasant. Fully fifty men have asked me to join their "outfits" in the Yukon country, so that they might have me for a pilot to the Klondike. I have kept clear of any such entanglements, however, up to the present time.

Hundreds of ready-made take-down boats, in six- and eight-foot lengths, have been brought to Alaska by Klondikers who expected to be able to portage them to the Yukon. These boats cost from $45 to $100 each, including freight, and are all being dropped and deserted along the trail.

One whimsicality of the camp has not been noted yet. I find every fellow who is able to do it is growing a beard. Most of them are scraggy-looking things at this time, being only three weeks old, but a few months more will make fierce-bearded men of the mountains out of most of the Klondikers.

Your correspondent is faring no better than anybody else. Young Eugene Grever, of Cincinnati, a chance acquaintance and a nice boy of 22, is my present companion. There is only one other Cincinnati man on the trail at present, Henry Prigger, and he is making money packing for other people.

My tent is a "9 by 9" and is crowded with bedding and provisions. On the floor as I sit writing is a sheet-iron Klondike stove which will never see the Klondike. My seat is a pile of blankets, and my backrest is a stick of wood. Between "packing" my horses, from morning to night, cooking meals and sleeping five hours out of twenty-four, I have had my hands more than full. We leave for Lake Bennett on the morrow. As soon as the struggle to get over the trail to the Yukon shall be ended, I will have time to write more fully of the experiences of the Klondikers. At present, every moment is of priceless value. Winter is almost upon us, and a long journey yet remains ahead.[2]

August 13, 1897

This morning I started for Lake Bennett with Heinz LeRoller and J. L. Waller. We had the two gray horses owned by E. Grever and me, and two dark horses belonging to the Waller outfit. One of our horses was packed with my personal effects and some provisions.

[2]This is Wells's last newspaper article prior to the time he reached Lake Bennett. His letters to the *Post* concerning that part of the trip were carried on the steamship *City of Mexico,* which was wrecked at sea, and all mails lost en route to Seattle. Fortunately, Wells also recorded the journey over White Pass in his journal, so that is the source of this account.

My camera and photographic apparatus were in the outfit. The job of throwing the Mexican hitch was undertaken by Waller.

As we advanced, the trail became extremely difficult and ofttimes quite dangerous. The thin covering of moss and earth had been disturbed by the hooves of the horses and in numerous places slanting surfaces of rock were exposed, down which the pack animals which we led were compelled to slide. This feat was made more hazardous by the narrowness of the trail, which, winding along the mountainsides, often followed dizzy precipices, over which a single misstep would throw man or beast. At one point we slid our horses successfully down a steep rocky incline, which turned abruptly away to the left along a precipice 300 or 400 feet high. At this place a horse belonging to Rice's packtrain had been dashed to death only the day before, falling upon the rocks far below. The utmost care was required in leading our horses, for negligence might at any time result in disaster. All four of the animals were remarkably surefooted, especially my two grays, which was all the more surprising in view of the fact that their previous mountaineering experience had been limited to hauling a grocery wagon up and down the inclined streets of Seattle.

The horses had cost $25 each in that city, while the feed bills and the freighting charges to Skagway had brought the total outlay on each up to $60 or thereabouts. At Skagway, I could easily have sold the two animals for $150 apiece.

At various points along the trail we caught brief glimpses of magnificent mountain scenery. There is something awe-inspiring about the gray angular peaks of the Northlands. Tall, gloomy and silent, they stand outlined against the steel-blue sky, an army of giants wearing chaplets of eternal frost and kilted from their waists down with the somber colors of the evergreens. The Arctic sun smiles coldly upon their serried ranks, while the rushing waters of the canyons and gulches breathe forth icy vapors.

August 14, 1897

We made our camp this evening beside some large boulders upon a mountainside. Here we made the unpleasant discovery that my lunch sack was missing. It had unperceived fallen from the packsaddle, having been loosely fastened. Waller volunteered to return four miles over the trail in hopes of recovering it, but his quest was in vain. The loss was a serious one, as our packs contained little besides flour and beans, without salt or baking powder to make bread. However, we were in for it and decided to make no grimaces.

Our course during this part of the trip lay up the Skagway River, a milk-white, foaming, cascading mountain torrent too deep in most places to wade and with water of freezing temperature. The trail crossed it several times on corduroy bridges.

Two surveyors whom we met at work with their instruments stated that they were in the employ of the Skagway Trading and Transportation Company and were running a preliminary line for a railway to the Yukon.

The forests which clothed the slopes of the Skagway Valley consisted almost entirely of scraggy spruce. White mosses were plentiful. The outcropping rocks appeared to be both igneous and slate.

August 15, 1897

This afternoon, having forded the Skagway River and climbed a steep mountain slope for fully a mile, we reached the summit of the Skagway pass and a few minutes later passed a small pile of stones which marked the boundary line between Alaska and British Columbia, as determined by the Canadian surveyors.

The so-called summit is really a long slough, or depression, between two parallel ranges of snow-capped mountains, and has an estimated altitude of 2600 feet. Numerous lakes and streams of small size, fed from the mountain snow, were seen. At first we observed the waters in this summit valley setting toward the Skagway River and Alaska. Then came a strip of country, perhaps half a mile wide, where the waters appeared stationary. Beyond, the rivulets began to flow in the opposite direction toward the Yukon; and then we knew, without consulting the surveyors' marks, that we were, according to the terms of the old Russian treaty, within the limits of the Queen's domain. Up to the present time no question has been raised as to the location of the boundary at this particular point.

The view spread out before us for many miles was wild and desolate in the extreme. It seemed, indeed, as though we had entered a forsaken world; were wandering, perhaps, among the peaks and ranges of the cold, lifeless moon. Gray billows of rock, fantastic and grotesque in shape, rose and fell far away to the horizon. Ponds and lakes embedded amidst the rocks revealed themselves here and there. Grass and mosses, mixed together, grew scantily along the trail. Few people were encountered after the first day. We had passed the main body of the Klondikers far behind and were now in the vanguard, pressing on toward the Yukon.

Only a few outfits of goods had reached the summit and the owners of these were plainly discouraged. Several of them were ready and willing to sell out to the highest bidder. One old Irishman stopped me with a proposition to buy one of my horses. "I'll give you four sacks of grub for one of them," he remarked. "We have only got one horse and he is about played out." This man then offered to sell his outfit on the spot for $1000 in cash and was clearly ready to leave the country.

On the evening of this day we camped at "the meadows," a swampy area where a wiry bunchgrass grew in considerable quantities. A detachment of the Canadian Northwest Mounted Police was stopping at this point for a few days and numerous horses were grazing nearby. A brilliant display of the Aurora Borealis was observed in the northern skies.

August 16, 1897

This morning Waller decided to return to Skagway with one horse, caching part of his goods at "the meadows," leaving LeRoller one animal to go ahead with me.

Our march this day lay through a country inexpressibly desolate, diversified only by rocks, ponds and streams of small size. There was no timber along the trail, but in the distance, on both sides, rose jagged granite peaks, spotted with patches of snow. We met few people. The sun was hot and a few mosquitoes appeared. No game was sighted.

At 11:40 A.M. we were passing through a patch of straggling spruce trees, the first outcroppings of the great forest that lay beyond, when we encountered a man named Frank Howard, a carpenter, who, with his partner, had come from Skagway to build a large freighting scow on Too-Shi Lake. They had been out eighteen days, had portaged 750 pounds of tools and provisions from Skagway on their backs, and only to make the discovery that Too-Shi Lake was not navigable and therefore the scow building would be useless. They had made a contract with the Skagway Trading and Transportation Company to build the scow for a good sum of money, but were now discouraged and ready to turn back. Howard's partner was away making a last effort to find navigable water at the lake. We were kindly furnished an excellent dinner of bacon, fruit, bread and coffee by Howard, who graciously accepted $2 for the food.

August 17, 1897

Our hike today consisted of traveling through open and forest lands, skirting several little lakes, and finally, pitching down the slope toward the Yukon Valley, we reached Lake Bennett about sundown, having met with no serious mishap. The trail from the "summit" to the lake had, in fact, been exceptionally good, with but one or two small muck spots.

At Lake Bennett, we found a motley array of tents upon the beach, perhaps fifteen in all, with half a dozen newly made boats drawn up on the sand or floating at anchor. We pitched our tent near one end of the line.[3]

Lake Bennett, B.C., Head of Yukon River, August 19, 1897

The much-vaunted White Pass to the Yukon is a failure. If Mr. White ever crossed by way of it he took an extra hazard of breaking his neck.

About one dozen men, including myself, have used the pass to reach the Yukon with outfits. Nearly 2500 others are struggling to accomplish the same feat, and it is believed that not more than two dozen will succeed before winter shall set in. The others will be stranded in the mountains.

I wish now, without loss of time, to send back a word of warning to everybody. Keep away from Skagway and White Pass, if going to Klondike. Avoid Dyea also, which is the entrance to Chilkoot Pass, and take steamship passage next spring for St. Michael, at the mouth of the Yukon, and then ascend the river on one of the regular boats. This is the only cheap and really practicable route at the present time.

At Chilkoot Pass the rush of Klondikers with provisions has produced a congestion which really amounts to a blockade. Little assistance can be secured from the Indians, as the latter are worn out from extra work and are slow to do more packing on their backs even at 35 cents a pound. The men who go over that pass are obliged to carry their own goods, which requires from six to nine

[3]This is the end of the journal entries describing this portion of the trip.

Wells took this photograph of his packtrain and companions approaching the summit of the final pass before reaching Lake Bennett, B.C.

weeks, depending upon the quantity of stuff. The work demands herculean efforts, and wears out all but the strongest men. The Chilkoot Pass is 26 miles in length.

A miner portaging 1200 pounds of provisions for the winter must make 12 round trips of 52 miles each, a total of 624 miles over precipitous mountains, carrying a 100-pound pack for that entire distance.

At Skagway, four miles from Dyea and the Chilkoot Pass, is the entrance to White Pass, and here the conditions are even worse. The pass has been advertised far and near as an available, easy route for packhorses.

A second view of the expedition approaching Lake Bennett, B.C.

Dr. George M. Dawson, of the Canadian Geological Survey and a recognized authority on geographical matters in the Northwest Territory, has stated that White Pass is the shortest and most available route to the Yukon gold fields. He gives its altitude at the highest point at 2600 feet above sea level, and declares that it is 36 miles in length, of which only 7 miles are difficult, the remaining stretches being easy grades.

Statements like this have been repeated and published so generally that many people have come to look upon the pass as a sort of asphalt boulevard from the seacoast to the Yukon. Hundreds of

Klondikers coming from "the States" have brought hand wagons with them, intending to wheelbarrow their goods over a route that would tap the energies of a mountain goat! One young fellow, whose name and asylum address cannot be ascertained, brought a bicycle to Skagway and started to carry it into the mountains. I passed the machine five days ago, hanging upon a rock five miles out.

The misinformation which has gone out concerning White Pass bears a most culpable imprint, inasmuch as it appears to have been published for a speculative and selfish purpose. The British Yukon Company, of London, through an American representative, secured control of the Skagway seafront, built a wharf and sawmill and then, it is claimed, announced to the world that it was ready to do business in the Yukon country over White Pass. Thousands of people, anxious to go to the Yukon, were misled by the announcements and purchased outfits of provisions, clothing, etc., before coming to Skagway. Most of them also brought horses.

Now these unfortunate people are in a trap at Skagway. The trail to the Yukon is almost impassable and is daily growing worse. The thin soil on the rocks has been mostly worn away by the hooves of the horses, leaving steep and dangerous slopes, down which pack animals can hardly slide without breaking necks or legs.

Dan Rice's packtrain of sixteen horses lost four animals which slid or fell over precipices during its last trip to the Yukon.

One strange feature of the situation at present is the fact that but few of the men who are striving to cross the mountains here realize as yet that they cannot succeed before winter comes. Most of them are handling their stuff by the relay system, packing it a few miles at a time, and are all unconscious of the vast distance yet lying between them and Lake Bennett.

Only a dozen or so outfits have been brought as far as the summit of the pass, although several thousands are in the mountains from 2 to 10 miles from Skagway.

When I came over the trail with my packhorses, I was hardly able to force a way for the first 5 miles, on account of the jam of horses, men and provisions, all headed toward the Yukon. A few miles out, however, the trail became comparatively clear, and 15 miles from Skagway it appeared to be but little traveled. A few outfits had been packed as far as the summit, 16 miles out, but I found the owners very much discouraged. Some of them had been out exploring on the trail and had discovered magnificent distances ahead.

Beyond the summit lies a rough, broken country extending 35 miles to Lake Bennett. The trail on this part of the route was finished only ten or twelve days ago, and is in a fairly good condition, compared with the first 16 miles.

The entire pass is 41 miles long, as shown by recent measurements, instead of 36 miles, as reported by surveyor Ogilvie and Dr. Dawson. So far from being an easy route to traverse, it is more difficult than Chilkoot Pass, owing to the number of summits, which are not shown on the prospectus.

There are three mountains to be climbed and descended before the one at the summit is reached. White Pass to the Yukon will never be available until a railroad shall have been built through the pass from Skagway. Such a road is feasible and is now in contemplation. In fact, I met two surveyors who were making a preliminary prospecting trip along the route.

No permanent horse trail can ever be constructed through White Pass, owing to the acute angle of the rock surfaces and the scanty soil with which they are covered.

The market price of horses in Skagway, which now averages from $150 to $175 per animal, will decline sharply within a few weeks when the Klondikers there discover their inability to reach the diggings this year by way of the trail. There will be many bitter disappointments, as many hundreds of the unfortunates have risked their all upon the venture. Others have been "staked" by good friends at home, and are loath to return and report failure. The outfits cost from $500 to $800 each, and in most cases will be a total loss. Thousands of tons of provisions will be left to waste in the mountains along the trail when the owners are driven out by the oncoming blasts of winter. Some men will undoubtedly stay with

42

their stuff and will suffer great hardships. The story of White Pass when complete will be full of sorrowful and tragic interest.

Lake Bennett, B.C., August 20, 1897

The morning after our arrival at Lake Bennett a trip to the sawmill, one mile distant, resulted in the disappointing discovery that the proprietors of same would take no more advance orders for skiffs. Messrs. Rudolph, Markus and Rocco had forty orders ahead, enough to keep them running until September 12, at the least. They were out of pitch and nails and did not know just when their messenger would return with some. He had gone to Dyea. Rudolph told me the only thing to do was to remain near at hand and after they got the pitch, etc., it might be possible for me to pick up a contract boat, provided it was not called for within three days after completion, as the rule required.

The boatbuilding industry on this lake is unique in many respects and well worthy of description.

About a year ago Rudolph, Markus and Rocco, three Juneau carpenters, conceived the idea of carrying a two-horsepower engine and boiler over Chilkoot Pass to the headwaters of the Yukon, in order to establish a small sawmill and build boats for the miners descending the river. Up to that time, every miner on reaching Lake Bennett or Lake Lindeman had been obliged to construct his own raft or a boat from whipsawed lumber.

The engine was portaged over the divide at great expense, and with infinite difficulty, and was finally erected on a small river emptying into Lake Bennett. The machinery, being driven by only two horsepower, was necessarily light, the saw being only 14 inches in diameter.

As soon as the "mill," standing out in the open air, got to working, it proved a remunerative investment. The miners preferred to buy boats rather than to whipsaw lumber, and Rudolph & Co.

received good prices for their work, which was of crude but strong character. They realized about $75 to $100 on each boat.

The rush of people to Alaska had not begun, however, and Rudolph and his partners had no premonitions of it. They laid in no supply of nails, pitch or oakum for the future. Suddenly the multitude of Klondikers appeared on the seacoast and couriers began to arrive demanding boats. Rudolph at once sent a man to Dyea and Juneau for pitch, oakum and nails, and took a large number of contracts for boats at advancing prices. A 1500-pound boat was quoted at $75, a 2500-pound boat at $90, a two-ton boat at $150 and a three-ton boat at $300.

The boats were warrantied to carry the number of pounds mentioned.

The prices quoted lasted up to a few weeks ago, when newcomers, seeing that they could not make arrangements with the mill for boats, began to offer fancy figures and prices took a jump. Now the mill is rushing its contracted boats in order to get the same out on time, and then if any more time remains, it will be able to command double and triple prices for boats. At Lake Lindeman, six miles above Lake Bennett, one Klondiker has been offering as high as $350 for a ready-made $90 boat. It is probable that just as the season is closing there will be scores of men on the lakes willing to pay any price for boats to descend the Yukon. It will then be too late to whipsaw lumber and the mill will be unable to supply the demands.

The skiffs or boats turned out by Rudolph, Markus and Rocco are made from green spruce lumber. The boards are one-half inch thick and average four knots to the foot. In fact, the knots make the lumber very inferior in quality and hardly fit for use for any purpose. But it is the best the country affords. The spruce grows to eight inches in diameter and branches close to the ground. Occasionally a ten-inch tree is found, but not often do they grow any larger.

The skiffs are built with sharp-pointed bows and wide sterns on flat bottoms. The sideboards are lapped, and the whole boat is caulked with oakum and heavily pitched to keep out the water. No paint is used to finish the craft, which are intended only for use in going down the river to the Klondike. The rays of the sun soon cause cracks to appear unless the boats are kept well saturated with water.

Rudolph has three men working with him besides his partners. One is the engineer, who receives $10 a day and his board. The other two employees do carpenter work on the boats at the same rate, $10 and board. One of these carpenters is a genial Missouri editor who left his wife to "run the paper" for a year while he went Klondiking. At present he is earning money for his outfit.

The "board" furnished employees by Rudolph is rather poor at present, consisting of beans, bread and tea, but it is the best the country affords. Rudolph has been unable to get in any supplies, but he is coining money.

The mill gets its lumber for nothing. Miners coming into the country without money to pay for a boat prefer to log for the mill, receiving a 25 percent share of all boards cut from logs which they cut and raft to the mill. Rudolph and his partners retain the other 75 percent of the boards for their own use.

Some Klondikers are whipsawing lumber and building boats near here, but the large majority avoid this heavy labor through the assistance of the mill. The lumber cut by Rudolph is nominally quoted at $100 per 1000 feet, but no one can purchase it at any cash price. Labor at logging is what the mill men want, and labor they get.

Having failed in my initial quest for a boat, I went back to camp determined to remain and secure one. When I announced my determination to LeRoller he made me a proposition to take my two gray horses with him back to Skagway and get Grever and 350 pounds of provisions and bring both to Lake Bennett, retaining the two horses as his pay. I accepted the offer and LeRoller left the next morning for Skagway with the horses to carry out his agreement, it being understood that he would return within a week's time.

Having now some days' leisure, I concluded to try seine fishing and so mounted my five-inch gill net on the beach. My neighbors were skeptical as to the outcome, no one knowing whether there were large fish in the lake or not. It was difficult to obtain assistance in preparing the net, although one man finally volunteered to tie knots for a while.

When the net had been duly mounted, I succeeded in getting it placed in the lake off a rocky point where two small rivers met. On the morning of August 20, a violent commotion among the cork floats of the net announced a capture, and we hastened out in our boat to secure the prize. It proved to be a four-pound whitefish, the shape and appearance being identical with that of the Lake Superior whitefish. The skeptics on the beach were amazed and I was overwhelmed with offers of assistance in setting the net, etc.

Encamped on the beach nearby was ex-police detective W. H. Welch of Portland, who was en route to Klondike. He informed me that a noted bank burglar had passed down the Yukon and that many other "good people" of rogue's gallery fame were daily embarking at Bennett for the gold diggings.

Reports of trouble on the Skagway trail began to come in thicker and faster as the days went by. One day it was announced that two men had been shot on the trail for stealing grub. Anarchy was reported. A terrible confusion existed, and men, horses and outfits were jammed in almost inextricable confusion. It was further stated that many pack animals had fallen over precipices or had become hopelessly mired and were shot.

Among the campers was an old Forty Mile Creek miner named McCloud, who had been on the beach since June with 2000 gallons of whiskey and a stock of dry goods, awaiting the return of his partner, Black Sullivan, who had gone to Victoria to secure a permit for the whiskey to enter the country. McCloud was tired of waiting and was in chronic ill humor.

Occasionally I visited the sawmill and witnessed the boatbuilding operations in progress there. Near the mill were numerous parties of miners constructing their own skiffs, either from whipsawed lumber or from boards obtained from the mill. The mill now had a number of carpenters at work for $15 per day plus board and was turning out boats as rapidly as possible, with little regard to proper bracing. Three boats per day was said to be the usual output, when nails and pitch were plentiful. These boats were constructed of rough five-eighth-inch lumber, not planed, and were unpainted when delivered to purchasers.

Lake Bennett, B.C., August 23, 1897

Flour is quoted here today at $35 per sack of 48 pounds, or a trifle over $140 per barrel.

It is very scarce and hard to obtain even at this price. Only three cannon shot away (40 miles) on the salt-water side of the mountains, flour can hardly be given away, although a few Klondikers have been able to sell the stuff for $1 per sack, or $4 per barrel. The difference in the price of flour at Skagway, on the seacoast, and at Lake Bennett, on the Yukon side, shows the enormous difficulty of overland transportation by way of either White Pass or the Chilkoot Trail. Other foodstuffs are correspondingly dear here.

Yet, despite these starvation prices, the country around this lake furnishes a native menu that would tempt an epicure. At a spot on the lake's front within a hundred yards of my tent I have been able within the last forty-eight hours to lay my hands upon freshly caught grayling, salmon trout, whitefish, wild duck, cranberries, blueberries and pineberries. No man need starve with a shotgun and fishing appliances during the summer at least. There are some delicious wild currants growing upon the mountainsides near by, and tracks of moose, caribou and silver-tip bears are plentiful three miles up a river canyon to the east.

Think of the St. Nicholas menu that, with the aid of a little of my $140 flour and baking powder, can be prepared if one but takes the time and trouble. Here is the card in plain English:

47

Menu, Hotel Scripps-McRae

Caribou Soup
Grayling, Fried or Baked
Trout, Fried or Baked
Whitefish with Cranberries

Fricassee of Wild Duck

Silver-tip Bear Steaks
Loin of Caribou
Moose Heart Boiled

Pancakes
Currant Pie
Blueberry Roll

Hot Water
Cold Water
Plain Ice

What do you think of it, anyhow?

Today I intend to have a blueberry pie and fried whitefish on the supper card. So far I have not taken the trouble to go up the canyon for silver-tip bear or caribou, but may do so in the course of a few days. The blueberry pie, valued at $35, is a certainty for tonight, however, as I have the blueberries in a pail in my tent, also the flour and the baking powder. There are also some beans worth $50 a sack under the pillow of my bed and seven pounds of bacon worth $1.50 per pound, which I borrowed from another man of generous heart. I have two ounces of tea in a can and some of Armour's extract of beef. I am fixed. What does a man need more?

Tonight my packhorses are on their last trip in, bringing provisions aggregating 300 pounds, which will cost me the two horses, valued at $300 for the pair. This 300 pounds of provisions will therefore cost $1 per pound for freighting over the trail. Prices are rising and flour may yet be worth $225 a barrel. These statements are no jokes. They are grim realities. It is due to the difficulties of getting into the country that such prices are possible. That is one reason so few Klondikers have reached Lake Bennett.

Yet while a man spends on the one hand with prodigal hand, if he possesses a fair degree of shrewdness, he makes on the other hand. I have managed by speculation and a rising market to clear 33 percent already on my cash capital in hand, and this within two weeks. There are chances on every hand to make from $10 to $30 per day if a man has the time and opportunity to take advantage of the same.

For instance, a person with the proper tools and a supply of nails, pitch and oakum can clear $50 per day here at present building skiffs. Three men are doing it. Nobody else has the tools or the material. Men who pack for others receive $10 per day and their board. Few want to work at any price for others. All are intent on reaching Klondike before the winter shall arrive.

Lake Bennett, B.C., August 23, 1897

Reliable men arriving here tell of terrible confusion and bloodshed along the Skagway trail. Two men, names unknown, were shot near Skagway yesterday for stealing provisions which had been carried by the owners partway on the trail. One of the thieves will probably die.

It is stated by others just arrived at this point that 5000 people are now in Skagway, most of them with horses, all intent on forcing their way across the pass before winter shall come.

The trail is now in a frightful condition, owing to the heavy traffic over it, and much trouble results.

A moderate estimate places 2500 horses upon the first six miles of the trail out of Skagway. These pack animals are continually meeting at narrow and dangerous places, and the drivers at once draw their revolvers and dispute the right-of-way. The cooler man of the two generally bluffs his antagonist, and the latter retreats with his horses and forces them to the outside of the trail, where they are in many cases pushed over the precipice and killed.

If a horse falls on the trail the drivers of animals behind either throw the animal from the cliff or drive, roughshod, over it. Fully fifty horses are killed or disabled every day along the trail and their packs are lost.

Thievery is growing to an alarming extent. Some men who cannot get their own stuff across the mountains are stealing sacks of provisions from the caches along the mountains, and are thus entering the Yukon. Such fellows will be killed hereafter whenever detected.

To add to the terrors of the situation along both the Skagway and Dyea trails, highwaymen and robbers from Montana, New Mexico and Arizona are putting in an appearance. Murders and robberies will soon become common unless these desperadoes shall be shot or hanged.

Winter is now but a few weeks away and the thousands of Klondikers in the mountains along the trails will be in a terrible plight.

It would not be amiss for the United States government to at once send a regiment of soldiers to Skagway to preserve order, protect lives and property and assist the unfortunate thousands who will be left struggling and perishing in the mountains. I am writing this dispatch in great haste to send back by courier passing my tent, en route to the seacoast.

I have sent numerous communications to the Cincinnati *Post* within the last two weeks, but fear that some of them have been lost. There is no regular mail service from Skagway as yet, and letters take chances of reaching the nearest post offices at Juneau, Seattle or San Francisco.

It is my belief that within the next ten days several thousand Klondikers along the Skagway trail will desert their outfits and make a mad run into the Yukon country, taking chances of starvation. I will be in the thick of the trouble and will send out the facts. Many unreliable reports emanating from Skagway newspaper reporters are being sent back to the United States. The writers are on the coast and have not even seen the Skagway trail or the Yukon. There will be little news that will escape me, both along the Skagway trail and in the Yukon this fall and winter.

Lake Bennett, B.C., August 24, 1897

The advance scouts of the army of Klondikers advancing into the Yukon country by way of White Pass are but few in number and grub is exceedingly scarce. Those of us, say three dozen, who have reached Lake Bennett recently have come through with light outfits, expecting our provisions to follow within a few days on packhorses.

Now, the truth of the matter is: I am here in my tent on Lake Bennett with three-fifths of a sack of flour—say 30 pounds—1⅛ pounds of baking powder and 37 pounds of dried peas. This stuff is all that I own in fee simple on this side of the mountains, except my photographic apparatus, bedding, clothing, medicines and a 75-foot gill net.

The net, however, is worth its weight in gold. I value it at present at $1200 cash and am not anxious to sell. It cost $8 in Seattle. The net is the only one on the upper Yukon, however, and is bringing me rich returns. It is equal to a Klondike claim. Other men on the beach are worrying themselves to death over a straight diet of bacon, and have no fresh meat or fish, although they possess dried fruit and sugar, flour, beans, tea and coffee—that is, some of them. So I have hit on a plan to secure relief.

I run a fish market on the lake. The net furnishes me daily magnificent Arctic trout and whitefish, weighing from four to nine pounds each. These fish I trade for sugar, tea, dried apples and the like. A cup of sugar secures one whitefish. A pound of apples is the purchase price of a trout.

I do not deliver the fish. Not much. The baconized man on the beach, who wants fish, goes out to my gill net by permission, secures fish, brings it ashore for my inspection and then goes to the tent, where his supplies are kept, and brings the purchase price in eatables.

How does this strike you for a bloated monopoly? It is no joke. The business is a serious one on both sides.

Today a Mr. McGee, one of the best-known real estate dealers in San Francisco, came to my tent and poked his head through the flap. McGee is worth a half million dollars in Frisco, but insists on going Klondiking for more gold. He is one of the baconized men who are hungry for fresh fish.

"I took a whitefish out of your net this morning," he remarked. "What do you want for it?"

"What have you got?" I demanded.

"Several things; state what you need."

"Dried fruit?"

"Yes, apricots. Fine as figs. I'll go and bring you some."

"That's all right. It's a bargain."

"Say, by the way," whispered McGee, "I saw another man taking fish from your net today. Did he pay?"

"No," I exclaimed. "Who was he?"

"The fellow in the fifth tent."

"Well, sir, it must be understood on the beach that the gill net is my property and grubstake. It is all I have to depend upon at present, except flour and peas," I replied decisively.

McGee went his way and rustled some elegant apricots. I am eating some of them now.

Lake Bennett, B.C., August 25, 1897

My sojourn on the lake is drawing to a close. For nine days I have been busily engaged here in making preparation for the descent of the Yukon River.

By dint of much persuasion and pressure I have been able to secure a boat from Rudolph, Markus and Rocco.

As soon as I reached this place and found how things were going I determined to camp and wait for a favorable opportunity to buy up a boat, as raft timber had been all culled out around the lake. My first visit to the little sawmill was unsatisfactory. Mr. Rudolph, the managing partner, said to me, "Your only chance is to buy some boat that has been ordered and not called for. A good many parties of men now attempting to cross the mountains with their outfits have sent couriers ahead with orders for boats and have made cash deposits on the same.

"Two-thirds of these parties will fail to get across in time to claim their boats when finished. I cannot hold the craft longer than four days after the same are contracted for, and if not then claimed the deposits will be forfeited and the boats sold. You see your chance."

I saw it and waited three days. Then I went again to the mill. Rudolph said, "Can't do anything for you at present. We have no more pitch or nails with which to build boats. Our expected supplies have not arrived over Chilkoot Trail."

"Suppose I rustle some pitch and nails, what then?"

"You can have a boat built at once, ahead of all contracts, while we are waiting."

I rustled. On the beach I met a man who had ten pounds of pitch for his own boat, which he was building himself from lumber cut by the mill. I made friends with the man with the pitch, and finally made bold to demand the loan of his priceless treasure until my own should arrive on the packhorses.

He looked me over carefully and deliberately. "That pitch is not for sale at any price. Three hundred dollars would not buy it," he said to me. "Are you sure that you have pitch coming?"

"I am sure," I replied, looking as earnest and solemn as the occasion required.

It was a desperate moment, that man with the pitch was hesitating.

"I'll give you $5 for the loan of the pitch three days," I finally exclaimed.

"Well, stranger, I'll accommodate you," my new acquaintance replied. "You're to return the pitch when yours arrives. I will also take the $5 merely as security, and will return it when I get my pitch back."

How I blessed that blessed man, who had enough confidence in me to loan twelve pounds of pitch with only $5 security! But I had no intention of "doing" him. My own pitch was really on the way, for I had sent special instructions to my traveling companion, Grever, at Skagway, to bring it with him.

Next I rustled for six- and eight-penny wire nails. Many inquiries along the beach proved fruitless. A few men had nails, but they would not sell at any price. Finally I struck the right fellow.

"Yes, I have four pounds of nails," he replied to my question, "and I am about to offer them to the mill for some bacon, as I want to start for Klondike without delay. I have no cash price to set on the nails. Money is no object. I want bacon."

"You shall have it," I replied confidently, although I had none to spare. "Don't let the mill have those nails."

"All right. Will be glad to accommodate you. Don't want to accommodate the mill. Bring out your bacon."

"How much?" I inquired furtively.

"Enough for me to go down the river."

I hurried away to the tent of a newly made acquaintance, "Montana Kid," the prizefighter.

"Kid, have you any bacon to loan?" I inquired.

"Yes, I'll accommodate ye," he replied after a moment's pause. "How much do you nade?"

"One whole piece!"

"Gee! So much? Will I git it all back?"

"Sure. I have some coming on my own packtrain."

"All right. Here's the stuff," remarked the Kid, handing me out an eight-pound piece. "It's all I've got, but I don't mind it now. Oim goin' fer that rascal Frinch, that hasn't packed me outfit over to the lake, and oi'll be away fer some days. Whin yours comes you can lave me a piece."

So I secured pitch and nails and descended once more upon the sawmill proprietors, carrying the precious articles. Rudolph was surprised and congratulated me. "You shall have a boat at once," he said. "It will be done in two days."

And he was as good as his word. He had the lumber ready and on Saturday evening a 26-foot spruce skiff was turned over to me in consideration of $90 cash. "You are getting that boat cheap," he remarked. "Other men are paying me $125 for the same kind of boat on contracts."

"But I furnished the pitch and nails!" was my reply.

Lake Bennett, B.C., August 26, 1897

Montana Kid, the prizefighter, has located his tent on the beach next to mine. The Kid is a formidable man, at both swearing and slugging, and is away from home at present on a warlike expedition. He took eleven men along with him from the beach, and vowed to pulverize and macadamize "Long Shorty French," a packtrain contractor, who has so far failed to bring over the outfits of the Kid and the eleven others, as per written contracts. The Kid has been reduced to straight beans and tea for three weeks, and has become decidedly wrathy. He declared before leaving to catch

French that the latter had been playing him and his friends false by packing goods for other men at higher prices.

The party of twelve avengers, including the Kid are reported to have overhauled Long Shorty and his packtrain yesterday ten miles from this point and promptly seized the culprit and the horses, dumped a Klondiker's outfit that was being portaged and are now marching on Skagway with Long Shorty and his eleven horses, intending to call on the miners for assistance, if necessary, to hold the packtrain and use it until their stuff shall all have been portaged to Lake Bennett, as per contracts. Then they will return the animals to Shorty.

Of course, the Kid and his friends will have to do their own packtrain work, as Long Shorty will hardly be willing to assist.

It seems he had agreed to pack their outfits across to the lake at 15 cents per pound, whereas the prevailing demand has raised the market rate to 40 and 50 cents per pound for large outfits, of $1 per pound for small quantities of goods. Naturally, Long Shorty wants to go back on his 15-cent contracts, but the Kid and his friends vigorously object.

The seizure of the packtrain has caused a sensation throughout this vicinity, but most persons say that the Montana Kid is right. There is no law in this region to compel respect for contracts, and the strongest man usually wins.

Lake Bennett, B.C., August 26, 1897

If Aunt Polly were here, what a picnic she would have borrowing tea, sugar and salt from the neighbors. I do not refer to your Aunt Polly, gentle readers, nor to my Aunt Polly, but to that typical Aunt Polly who lives partly by purchasing supplies from the grocery and partly—a big partly—by borrowing next door. This is the place for her to live. Here it is the style for everyone to borrow. If one wants a piece of bacon he borrows it from the inhabitants of the next tent.

Ten minutes later the fellow who loaned the bacon will probably come and borrow your sheet-iron stove or your coffee pot. A Scandinavian will next appear and ask for the loan of a couple of handfuls of beans until his packhorses arrive. Next Peter McCloud will step over from his tent and ask if you have a teaspoonful of baking powder to spare till his packtrain comes over the hill.

And so it goes. We all borrow and live, basing our transactions upon the hoped-for arrival of our provisions from over the divide.

Ex-Judge Osborn, of Seattle, just in on the lake by way of the Dyea trail, will be borrowing by tomorrow. Probably he will find that he left his snuff box at home, or that his wife forgot to put a darning needle in his kit.

The Judge brought in several hundred pounds of dignity with him, but he will lose it all before he has been Klondiking for two months. It isn't conducive to dignity to sit in the sand, with cinders and smoke flying in one's face, and holding a frying pan full of bacon over the fire.

Here I am, sitting on a piece of dirty canvas in a tent, with a sack of beans for a backrest and a miscellaneous assortment of biscuits, bacon, medicine, sugar and stewed apricots piled up *en négligé* on my left. In front of my tent are swinging two towels, which, for the life of me, I have been unable to boil clean in the hot-water kettle.

I rubbed the black, sooty bottoms of several cooking utensils with those towels, and the soot seems to have stained them like indelible ink.

An intelligent young lawyer is attempting to make bread fifty feet or so to leeward. While I think he knows the duties of his profession fairly well, it would go hard with him to attempt to hold a kitchen job in Cincinnati at $2.50 per week.

There is an ex-detective from Portland, named Welch, a few yards further down the beach, who makes considerable pretensions as a cook, but he overreached himself by trying a currant pie. He gathered the wild currants all right just back of town, but he quit when the pie-dough proposition stared him in the face.

A young dry-goods clerk came to my tent last night, cold and hungry. His side whiskers and curly brown hair both had a ragged uncut appearance. His blue overalls and Klondike boots were covered with mud.

He was wet to the skin from traveling over the Skagway trail all day in the rain. He was sick and miserable and unable to cook. I got him a lunch. This morning he wanted to make pancakes, and naïvely inquired if he must put shortening in them. Dear boy, I think he supposed that the butter crock or the lard can was standing on the shelf just inside my tent.

A big, fleshy dentist named Van Sant,[4] apparently 50 years of age, hailing from Peoria, Illinois, told me last night that he had left his wife and four assistants in charge of his business and had quietly come Klondiking without letting anybody know it except the aforesaid wife. "I'm off on vacation, so the public believes," said the dentist to me. Later on this gentleman of the forceps wanted to buy pitch off me, so that he could caulk his boat. He pleaded so earnestly for it that I made a partial promise to deliver when my pitch arrives on the packhorse.

Up at the head of Lake Lindeman, six miles from here, a Pacific Coast lady, Mrs. Fancheon, and her husband are camped with about 120 other people. The woman is small, bright, pretty and not over 35 years of age. She is attired in a complete outfit of male clothing, even to the pantaloons, and is full of push and enterprise.

Evidently she has full charge of the present family expedition, as she purchased a skiff yesterday for $325 cash and is now at work organizing a party of passengers to go downriver in it and help pay her expenses. Mrs. Fancheon is in the Yukon country to get a financial standing in the world, and unless luck is dead against her she will succeed.

There are numerous good stories told of this good little lady and her adventures on the trail from Dyea to Lake Lindeman. At one

[4]This is Wells's first mention of Dr. Van Sant. He later entertains Van Sant at Dawson. For Van Sant's account of his own experiences Klondiking, see Appendix I.

point, where a small creek was to be crossed, a Scotchman with a boat was ferrying passengers at 50 cents apiece and was making from $30 to $40 per day. Mrs. Fancheon came along unattended and entered the skiff. At the end of her trip, the ferryman demanded half a dollar.

"What's that you say?" exclaimed the fair passenger, drawing her revolver. "Do you mean to rob me? I'll never pay half a dollar to you for crossing this creek. You're a brigand, sir!" And with that parting shot the lady marched away, still carrying her gun in her hand. Now the boys on the trail are making life weary for that Scotchman.

Lake Bennett, B.C., August 27, 1897

Fresh snow which has fallen on the mountains along White Pass has badly scared the thousands of Klondikers who are struggling to get across the divide.

Many are dropping their outfits on the trail and are fleeing toward Skagway, believing that winter is near at hand. The majority, however, with anxious, pallid faces, are still pressing on, hoping almost against hope that fair weather will continue long enough to enable them to reach Lake Bennett and escape down the river to Klondike before ice closes navigation.

A three days' wind-, rain- and snowstorm prevailed on Monday, Tuesday and Wednesday in the mountains and caused terrible suffering. Few of the Klondikers were prepared with either clothing or blankets for the semi-blizzard, and hundreds fell victim to the elements.

Nearly all were soaked to the skin, sleeping in their wet clothes at night, without fires and chilled to the very marrow. Few had anything to eat except cold pocket lunches and the misery can better be imagined than described. Toiling hard all day, lying out in wet clothing and blankets at night, the seeds of fatal disease have been sown in hundreds of human beings who were caught in the turmoil of the elements.

The troubles and disasters which I predicted some time ago in my dispatches are already coming to pass. As the sun retreats southward, reddens and sinks beneath the horizon, and the Arctic winter comes whirling down from the north, scores, perhaps hundreds, of the brave men who are struggling across the mountains and down the icy rivers will be caught. Then in the gathering gloom of the chill Yukon twilight a grim tragedy will be enacted, witnessed only by the prowling wolves and recorded by naught save scattered bones.

Do not think this picture overdrawn. I know the country and know whereof I speak. The Yukon in winter is a death trap for the imprudent and inexperienced man, whether he be city-bred or mountain-born. The story of the Klondike will yet be written in human blood.

Barney McGee, an Irishman, who occupies the next tent to mine, returned to camp last night very much disheartened. He had, with one companion, been out on the summit of the Dyea trail when overtaken by the three days' storm. The two men pitched their tent in a small gulch in the rocks several miles above the timber. On the first night of the storm they slept comfortably enough, but on the second, about 3 A.M., they were suddenly awakened by a rush of waters which swept over them fully a foot in depth and carried down their tent.

The two unfortunates hastily fled with their blankets to an adjoining rock, upon which they perched, wet to the skin, throughout the long, cold hours that followed, while the flood, now of considerable size and velocity, swept by them down the canyon.

Barney, in describing his experience, said to me, "If I had been home I should have died shure. There we sot on the rock, near the top av of the mountain, wid our clothes wet as if we had been in the river, wid th' rain a fallin' and the wind a blowin' an' dark as the ace ov spades. Faith, an' thar wasn't a stick of wood nearer'n

60

two miles away, an' we couldn't light a foire. I thought I should die there waitin' fer mornin'."

Within half a rifle shot of my tent an ex-railroader with a wooden leg is camped. His name is Rugg, and he was thirteen years ago a brakeman on the Jersey Central Railroad. Falling under a car, he lost both his left leg and his job. Rugg then came West. He decided to attempt mountain hunting, and actually made an expedition among the Cascades after deer and mountain sheep.

Recently the stories of Klondike so interested Rugg that he decided to try his luck in the Yukon country, and accordingly started by the short and difficult route from Dyea over Chilkoot Pass to Lake Lindeman. He had with him when he landed at Dyea $116, less the cost of 400 pounds of flour, beans and bacon, which he had purchased for $30, and was determined to portage over the divide.

Away he stumped over the rocks, picking his way with the wooden leg and carrying a 60-pound pack on his back. He made short trips, relaying his outfit from point to point. Occasionally he would stop for a few days and act as cook for some party of Klondikers, thus making a few dollars. On one occasion he found a ferryman drunk at one of the rivers on the trail and took his job for three days, making a profit of about $50.

Having grown opulent by reason of his business successes, Rugg next hired a white man to help him carry his stuff for the remaining distance to Lake Lindeman. He joined a party preparing to descend the Yukon, paid for his share in the boat and today still has $10 in his pocket and hope in his heart.

Rugg and his newfound friends will set sail tomorrow for Klondike. He is an instructive example to the hundreds of tenderfeet who have two feet and who have failed to cross the Yukon because of wind, rain and discouragements. Rugg is apparently 45 years of age, bronzed, bearded, blue-eyed and blithe.

Wells's photograph of the boatbuilding "industry" at Lake Bennett, B.C.

Lake Bennett, B.C., August 29, 1897

A terrible panic is prevailing on the Skagway trail leading to Too-Shi Lake. Fully 2000 Klondikers, frightened by the appearance of heavy snows, freshly fallen upon the mountains, are attempting to escape to the seacoast, while others, perhaps 500 in number, are still pushing this way, determined to do or perish.

The jamming of men, horses and provisions on the trail, caused by these two opposite movements, has caused a confusion that beggars description. It is something frightful. Men with blanched faces, drawn and pinched from exposure and suffering, in wet clothes, stagger slowly along under huge packs, leading one or two horses heavily loaded and half starved, which slip and fall every few hundred yards and are unable to recover their feet without help.

The trail is so overcrowded between Skagway Hill and the foot of the "Summit Hills," 12 miles distant, that the opposing streams of men and horses are compelled to pass each other at certain places where waits of two and three hours are of frequent occurrence.

The trail, owing to six days of drizzling rain, has become so murky as to resemble a pigpen. Men and horses sink to their knees in the mire in many places. Slanting rock surfaces, from which the moss and soil have been completely worn, offer treacherous footing, and many horses tumble and slide down these places, breaking their necks or legs. The trail is strewn with festering carcasses of pack animals, and the atmosphere is filled with a terrible stench.

Here and there a horse will be seen, still alive, sunk in the mire up to his shoulders or neck, and left to die by the unfeeling owner, who would not even waste pistol bullets to put the brute out of its misery. Few of the animals have sufficient feed, and many are dying of actual starvation. Fully 600 horses have perished along the trail up to the present time, and thousands more will meet a similar fate.

The general panic prevailing has developed the brute instincts of the men themselves to an incredible degree. Few will assist their fellows in distress. It is a case of everyone for himself.

Along the trail are men without cooked provisions, bedding or even tents. They apply in vain for food or shelter to those who are fortunate enough to have either. It seems incredible, but hundreds of incidents are reported during the period of six days' rain just ended, wherein men, separated from their outfits and provisions, have begged and pleaded in vain for a cup of coffee, a piece of bread or the shelter of a tent.

They were obliged to sit out in the driving storm, while other men, one or two to a tent, slept calmly a few feet away. "We have worked hard and don't want to be crowded," was the usual surly answer to petitions for shelter.

(From a Photograph.)

The Post's Klondike Correspondent, E. Hazard Wells, making blueberry pies at his camp on the shore of Lake Bennett. [See Mr. Wells' last preceding letter.]

This is the version of Wells's photograph of his camp at Lake Bennett that the Cincinnati Post *ran. The technology for printing photographs in newspapers did not exist at the time, so engravers would make a line drawing on a plate to be stamped into the papers. For the most part, the line drawings were faithful to the original; however, in this instance, Wells's original photo apparently lacked the impact his editors were looking for, so they took it upon themselves to "spruce it up."*

Wells's photograph of his camp at Lake Bennett, B.C. (identity of the two men is unknown, but they are probably Heinz LeRoller and J. L. Waller, who accompanied Wells from Skagway to Lake Bennett).

65

JACK FROST CLOSES THE GATES TO THE LAND OF GOLD.

A Cincinnati Post *artist's rendering of "Jack Frost" (winter) closing the gates to the Yukon.*

BEFORE AND AFTER TAKING.

FATE THAT MAY BEFALL MANY A SEEKER AFTER GOLD WHO GOES TO THE KLONDIKE.

Another Post *artist's cartoon depicting the hard lesson learned on the Klondike by many of the gold seekers.*

One poor fellow told me that he offered $2 for a cup of coffee and was curtly refused. Another proffered a $5 gold piece for a biscuit, but in vain.

"Provide for yourself, or freeze or starve," is the unexpressed, but prevailing, sentiment. It is inhumanity in its worst form.

Two old men, gray-haired and bent, sat crying beside a muck hole. In it were their two horses, mired and helpless. Hundreds of men passed them a little to the right, and not one offered assistance. Not even a look of pity or sympathy was bestowed upon the unfortunates. The craze for gold had steeled the hearts of those who were once human beings.

During the last four days sections of the Skagway trail have been closed for temporary repairs by companies of men armed with rifles. Persons with packhorses who appeared on the trail were ordered to stop and go to work. In the face of the leveled rifles they could not refuse, and in this way thousands of workers were secured to wield the ax and shovels in filling up the muck holes. This policy is to be followed hereafter whenever any part of the trail becomes absolutely impassable.

Lake Bennett, B.C., September 3, 1897

This morning the trim little boat *Maude* set sail down the Yukon, bearing your correspondent and four other men toward Klondike. We expect to arrive at Dawson within two weeks.

The *Maude* is my personal property, and I put a high valuation upon her. Built at the Lake Bennett sawmill of rough-sawed green spruce timber, she is 26 feet long by 6 feet wide amidships, and has a carrying capacity of two tons. A square sail, 10 by 12 feet and rigged to a jury mast, will serve as a means of propulsion, assisted in calm weather by a pair of roughly hewed oars.

My traveling companions, all gold hunters, are Frank Walthers, of Seattle; John Duffy, of Montana; S. W. Foote and George Fulk, both residents of the state of Washington. Duffy and Foote are veteran mining prospectors. The others are city-bred men who have followed various pursuits. A portion of my outfit has failed to arrive on the lake, although packhorses were sent for it, and the stuff must be sacrificed unless by some lucky chance it shall be brought down the river after me.

The outfits in the *Maude* aggregate nearly two tons of provisions and baggage. We have several rifles and shotguns aboard and will keep an eye out for moose and caribou along the Yukon. Fish will also be secured with a gill net at Lake Marsh.

It is unsafe to delay longer at Lake Bennett, as winter is close at hand. The Skagway trail, which has been in a bad condition for some days, has become almost impassable and several thousand gold hunters, with their outfits, now caught upon it, are in a pitiable plight. There is a complete demoralization among them. A few are pressing vainly onward, but the large majority, sick at heart and discouraged, are abandoning their outfits and are retreating toward Skagway. Hundreds are broken in health from the terrible hardships and exposure to which they have been subjected during the nine days' rainstorm just closed, and many will undoubtedly die from pulmonary diseases thus contracted. Pitiful stories are told me hourly.

At one place on the trail are camping a man and his wife. They are stranded in the mountains, with their outfit, unable to proceed or retreat without abandoning it. The husband is a poor man and in despair. His wife spends her time in weeping. The couple have four small children in Seattle, Washington, left there with relatives. The entire family fortune has been spent upon the Klondike venture, and now all is lost.

Other men have mortgaged their homes; many have thrown up good situations; others again have sold out their businesses in the cities to embark on the Yukon mining speculations, and all are caught like rats in a trap on the Skagway trail. Ruin, desolation and despair brood over the region today, and many are the muttered curses, the tears and the vain regrets. The men who have reached the Yukon over Skagway, or White Pass, trail are few in number, perhaps sixty all told, while fully 10,000 have tried it and have been foiled and compelled to retreat.[5]

September 1, 1897

After I had secured my boat for $90, it would have been an easy matter to have sold it to one of the newcomers for $200 cash. Scores of men came to the mill and were refused contracts for boats at any price. They succeeded, in some cases, in purchasing whipsawed and mill boats for $200 and $300 each. Some of the men camped along the lake, seeing how things were going, and began whipsawing lumber to sell, receiving 40 cents per square foot for one-inch boards. Other men, who had intended to buy mill boats, sent back to Skagway for tools and prepared to cut timber and build their own craft.

In the meantime the price of horses at the Lake Bennett end of the trail fell to $75 a head, while the rate at Skagway continued to be $150 and $175 per animal. News reached us that town lots at Skagway were selling from $150 to $1500 each, the only title being possession of the ground. Steamers were still reported to be arriving daily, and more than 7000 people were now "in town."

LeRoller and Grever did not come, and fresh snow began to appear upon the mountain crests nearby. The nights were getting longer and darker. The air was crisp and cold after sundown. I man-

[5]The "almost impassable" condition of the Skagway trail as Wells departed for Dawson resulted in no mail being sent or received from the Klondike for most of the next two months. So the articles Wells sent to the *Post* describing his trip down the Yukon were never received, and no word whatever was heard from him from the beginning of September until the end of October. The following partial account is taken from Wells's personal journal.

aged to keep warm by sleeping in my fur parkie and sheepskin sack.

Camped near me on the beach was the Montana Kid and several friends. These men were vainly awaiting the coming of their outfits by packtrain. Finally, growing desperate, they started out, under the leadership of the Kid, to capture said packtrain, wherever it might be found, take the animals to Skagway and portage over their own outfits according to a long-standing contract. The train was duly captured and taken to Skagway, but the miners there refused to stand by the Kid and his friends and the scheme fell through. Then the Kid returned to Lake Bennett and embarked for Klondike, taking little food, except part of an outfit intended for someone else who had gone on ahead.

As weeks passed, hundreds of men embarked at Lakes Bennett and Lindeman and passed down into the Yukon. Much of the time it rained, and the discomfort and suffering was indescribable. Among the newcomers at the lakes were a number of sporting women en route to Dawson City. There were also numerous professional gamblers.

Lawyers, dentists, doctors, merchants, laborers and clerks, all are represented on the beach. There were but a few old-time miners on hand.

MEMORANDUM

Sand and dirt in tents, grub, everywhere. George Allen, son of U.S. Senator Allen, has sold outfit at the Meadows for $200. He and companion had two horses which died of starvation. Allen had a good outfit. His age—19; companion—21. Holdup of three days on the trail. Men with rifles compel each packer to pay $10 per horse or go to work fixing trail for two days.

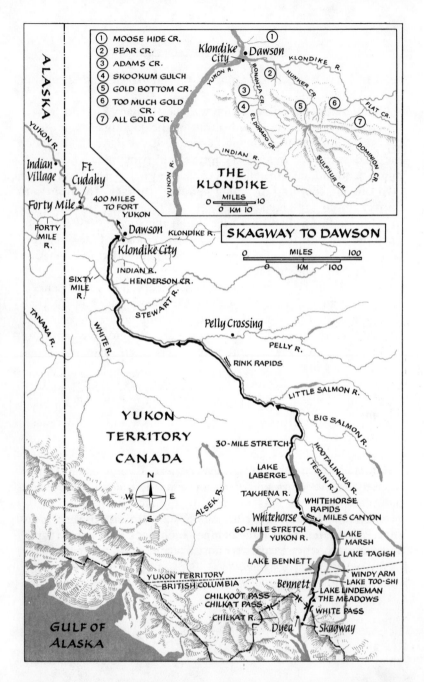

This map shows the "Gold Rush Trail" from Skagway to Dawson. Inset is the Klondike Mining District.

September 3, 1897

On September 3, 1897, I started on the trip down the lakes and Yukon River for Klondike. Grever and LeRoller had not arrived and I did not think it wise to wait longer for them. Word had reached me from LeRoller that he was struggling to get through on the trail, but it seemed very doubtful as to whether or not he would succeed. As for Grever, I could get no definite information. A rumor said he had gone home.[6] No answer came from him in response to three letters sent back over the trail and I was nonplussed as to what had really become of him.

Before deciding to start September 3, I had made arrangements to transport in my boat as passengers Frank Walthers of Seattle, and Sam Foote, George Fulk and John Duffy. The latter had only received a small part of his outfit, but the others were well provided, Walthers having 1,600 pounds, and Foote and Fulk about 900 pounds apiece.

When the outfits were loaded into the *Maude,* we discovered that the weight was almost too much for the boat, only six inches of freeboard being above the water. However, there was no time to alter arrangements and we started, intending to stop whenever bad weather prevailed.

A dreary light rain fell all day and a head wind prevailed, but we slowly made way with the oars down the lake. That night we camped about five miles from our starting point under the lee of a rocky bluff.

Subsequently, I learned that LeRoller, with my stuff on one horse, had arrived at Lake Bennett three hours after our departure.

On Sunday, September 5, we remained in camp. A heavy head wind from the north was blowing and a dangerous sea running. Fresh snow was observed on the mountains. In the evening we set our gill net off a rocky point.

[6]For once, the "rumors" were true. Grever had left the mountains and headed home via Skagway and Seattle.

On Monday, September 6, we found two fine trout and one whitefish in the net, averaging about four pounds each. The weather was cold and considerable sea was running, but there were breaks in the clouds and we got underway, ferrying our outfits across to the other side of the lake in two loads. We then edged up seven miles along the shore, finding the waves altogether too high for comfort, and finally went into camp, under a clear star-lit sky.

September 7, 1897

We saw the sun rise for the first time in two weeks this morning. The clouds had almost disappeared. We rose at 4 A.M. and were underway before 6 A.M. This day we made fine progress, leaving Lake Bennett and with a favoring wind sailing through Lakes Aares and Tagish. On "Windy Arm" we encountered a heavy sea and, being obliged to put out a long ways from land, were in considerable peril for an hour or more. The large waves chasing us astern threatened to come aboard, but by dint of hard rowing and sailing we managed to keep up a sufficient speed to travel nearly as fast as the waves. Sam Foote, who was an old sea fisherman, took the steering oar and occasionally he would beat off the tops of big combers coming up behind. Several of them washed up even with the stern of the boat. We all breathed more easily when we got across this exposed place.

We estimated our progress this day at 30 miles, our camp being pitched just inside of Lake Marsh.

Just before leaving Lake Tagish we came in sight of a flagpole displaying the British colors. Two tents were noticed on the beach. As we came abreast two men appeared and in response to our shout of inquiry stated that we must come ashore, as it was the Customs House for the region.

As we drew near the beach one of the men in hip boots waded out to the boat. He was Chief Officer Godson. The waves pitched

This is the photo Wells took from the bow of the Maude *as he and his companions passed through Miles Canyon (or the "Grand Canyon of the Yukon," as Wells called it) on September 9, 1897.*

us about considerably while he asked a few questions of each man concerning his outfit and hastily made out customs receipts. No charges were made for broken sacks of provisions in use or for hardware or clothing in use. Rigid examination of the boat was not made. In fact, nothing was disturbed, the statements of each man being considered final. The duty assessed was 25 percent on groceries and a haphazard percent on other things. The total for Walthers amounted to $18; Foote, $7.50; Fulk, $7.50; Duffy, nothing; Wells, nothing. Godson stated that he had received instructions from Ottawa to be easy on the miners.

On Wednesday, September 8, we left our camp on Lake Marsh at 6:15 A.M., and with a favoring breeze ran across the lake and 10 miles down the Yukon River, assisted by a three-mile current. The water in the river was at a high stage. No other boats were seen this day. We camped on a riverbank where an eddy made a convenient landing place. Walthers here caught two grayling. The gill net was set overnight, but brought no fish the next morning.

Thursday, September 9, we left camp at 6:15 A.M., the sky being overcast. At 11 A.M., we reached the entrance to the Grand Canyon and went ashore to survey the place. I had been through the canyon on a raft in 1889, but had not visited the spot since. Several other boats arrived soon after we went ashore. A survey of the canyon, which was seven-eighths of a mile long, determined us to run it with half a load of provisions, etc. Foote took the steering oar, Walthers and Fulk the oars, and I stood in the bow with a pole for emergencies and my camera poised and ready for a shot as soon as we reached the worst waters.[7]

[7]Inexplicably, and unfortunately, this is where Wells's account of the trip from Lake Bennett to Dawson ends in the journal. The next correspondence Wells sent was an article dated September 23, 1897.

PART II

ON THE KLONDIKE

Dawson, Northwest Territory, September 23, 1897

Tonight I send you my first message from the Land of Gold. The stories published of the fabulous wealth of the Klondike are true.

The half has not been told.

No such deposit of the golden metal was ever before discovered, at least in modern times.

A thousand, yes, 1200 claims on the Klondike and its tributaries are paying the owners princely tribute, and as far up on the benches and even the mountainsides as prospectors have gone the metal is found.

I do not send back the news with the intention of creating a stampede to the Klondike. Too many American citizens have already mortgaged their homes or have borrowed money from their friends and are overrunning this district, which is only 40 miles square.

Every available bit of ground on the Klondike and its tributaries has been staked off and recorded and is now being worked. There are no pickings left for newcomers, except on other rivers and creeks which have not yet been prospected.

The Klondike now contains 6000 to 8000 men and fully 2000 more are heading this way down the Yukon.

From the river's mouth it is rumored that other thousands are traveling hither on steamboats. If they should all arrive before the Yukon closes, fully 12,000 people will be on the ground to watch the 1200 Klondike claim owners taking out gold. It may be a pleasing occupation to watch these 1200 nabobs at work in the sands, but will it pay?

There is, moreover, a grave danger threatening. Dawson is short of provisions, and unless additional supplies arrive by the river steamboats within a few days, the ice will cut off all relief until June 1898.

In this case, the starvation of hundreds of people is possible. I make this statement guardedly. There is widespread alarm already over the situation among those who have no outfits of provisions. This alarm is growing more general as day after day the expected steamboats fail to arrive and the open season draws to an end.

The three trading posts or stores, belonging to the Alaska Commercial Company, the North American Trading and Transportation Company and Billy Burns, have sold out their entire stocks of flour, beans, rice, bacon, oatmeal, lard, butter, etc., and have but small remaining stocks of canned goods, sugar, tea, etc.

There are in round numbers 2000 people here who have as yet secured no supplies for the coming eight months of Arctic winter, and what they will do in case the steamboats fail to arrive before the ice closes navigation God only knows. The Yukon may be frozen over within a week, or it may keep open for three weeks longer, but the time is growing dangerously short.

Numbers of old and experienced Yukon miners, who are afraid to take chances, are hastily gathering up five-week grub outfits and are starting to "pole out" up the Yukon to Juneau and escape from the country. If the steamboats arrive all will yet be well. If not?

Men coming to the Yukon next spring should bring in provisions for at least one year. If the anticipated rush of gold seekers shall occur the trading companies will be utterly unable to supply the necessary rations, and a terrible winter will follow in 1898–99. A fund of $500 cash to the man, in addition to his outfit, is also desirable, as there are many heavy additional expenses to be met.

Those coming should also understand the nature of their venture. They risk all in prospecting new country. The chances are that two men will fail to make "strikes," while the third man will be successful. Even now in Dawson City there are over 300 disgruntled and disgusted men who are seeking the first easy and quick method of leaving the country. They will sail on the first steamer out.

Dawson, N.W.T., September 23, 1897

Through the courtesy of E. D. Bolton, Assistant Gold Commissioner of the Yukon District, I have been furnished with the first authentic statement of the gold claims recorded to date in this vicinity. The sum total of the claims is over 1000, distributed as follows:

In the Klondike division, which includes the Troandik River and tributaries:

	Claims
Bonanza Creek	189
El Dorado	55
Hunker Creek	148
Bear Creek	51
Adams Creek	27
Gold Bottom Creek	52
Nugget Gulch	5
Skookum Gulch	42
Homestake Gulch	16
All Gold Creek	60
Boulder Creek	20
Too Much Gold Creek	24
Fox Creek	4
Isaac Creek	15
O'Neill Gulch	7
Total Klondike	715

In the Indian Creek division:

	Claims
Sulphur Creek	148
Dominion Creek	70
Eureka Creek	50
Quartz Creek	2
Total Indian Creek	270

In other divisions:

	Claims
Bryant Creek	45
Montana Creek	41
Moose Hide Creek	35
Deadwood Creek	60
Henderson Creek	35
Stewart River	2

Grand total of gold claims in all divisions of the Yukon District is 1203.

No record is made of Forty Mile Creek claims, as that locality has been practically deserted. The same is true of Sixty Mile Creek and Miller's Creek.

The Dominion government opened its office for the recording of claims in Dawson on June 1 of this year, and it is expected that fully 1800 claims will be filed before January 1, 1898.

The Chief Commissioner is Thomas Fawcette, his assistants being E. D. Bolton and James Gibbons.

The fee for recording a claim is $15, which is good for one year, a renewal of the record costing $100 for each subsequent year. No miner's license is required.

So far no royalties, or other tax, except for recording, have been imposed upon miners. Gulch claims are 500 feet long from base to base of hill. Bench claims are 100 feet square.

After filing on a claim a miner holds it by being represented (either in person or by substitute) and working the same any three contiguous months in each year, the year dating from the time of recording the claim.

For instance, J.B. files on a gulch on September 23, 1897. He can be absent for the succeeding nine months, but must appear either in person or by substitute 90 days prior to September 23, 1898, and work the claim; or J.B. can come, say, in May, June and July, if he chooses, and do the necessary work.

Or he may choose October, November and December, or any other contiguous months.

It is well to make these facts clear, as so many false reports have been spread regarding the matter. There are no restrictions imposed upon United States citizens. They stand upon the same footing as Canadians, and have equal privileges.

Some of the newcomers, finding all the available claims in this district taken up, have left to explore new localities and to prospect new ravines and gulches. These men will endure many hardships in the next few weeks, and most of them will be likely to return to Dawson soon after the Arctic winter shall have set in in earnest.

Many believe that rich gold fields exist throughout a region not less than 200 miles long, of which the Klondike is the heart. Not a few also argue that the Arctic zone is the native home of gold, and beneath the foreign soil, on hill and in dale, from the mouth of the Mackenzie to Bering Strait, lie untold fortunes for those who shall come to claim them.

But these are theories not yet proved by exploration and are worthless except as theories. What we do know is the marvelous richness, the unexampled wealth in the fields in the locality about Dawson.

It is fairly to be expected that gold will be discovered elsewhere in this or a yet higher latitude, but it will be time enough to write about that when the discoveries shall have been made and the claims filed and worked.

October 3, 1897[1]

My newspaper communications, sent out to the Cincinnati *Post*, have been as frequent as circumstances would permit, and have been written under great disadvantages, amidst rain, cold and sleet. Sometimes my fingers were so numb I could scarcely hold a pencil. It was a wild, desperate rush to get here before the winter set in and cut me off. Now I am in Dawson and installed in a friend's cabin, ready for newspaper and photographic work. I took a number of pictures on the way down the Yukon, which I have not as yet had the opportunity to develop, but will do so, if possible, tomorrow.

Please deny for me that story that I discovered the Klondike in 1891 and staked off the best claims in the country. The absurd thing is following me even out here. I heard yesterday that a Seattle newspaper, just arrived, contained a statement that W. J. Arkell had sold his "rights of discovery" in the Klondike to a New York syndicate. As for me, I did not discover the Klondike and did not stake off claims in it. Glave was not on the Klondike at all, nor was Schanz.[2] I carried Schanz, while sick, past the Klondike on a raft to Forty Mile Creek, and he never came back up the Yukon to the Klondike.

The Associated Press interviewed me at Lake Bennett about the matter, and I tried to straighten out the tangle concerning Glave and me, but it seems that the story will not down. Get the *Post* to deny it emphatically, if it is still in circulation in "the States."

I want to have the truth told. The story seemed so ridiculous to me when it was sprung, just on the eve of my departure for Alaska, that I paid no attention to it. Since then I find that it has been published throughout the United States, and has attracted a great deal of attention. If some big stock gambling scheme is on, I wish to have my name disconnected with it at once. While I would be glad to make a fortune, it cannot be that way.

[1]This segment is a personal letter from Wells to his family.
[2]Schanz and Glave went to Alaska with Wells on his second trip, in 1890–91.

Of all the strange experiences of my life this Klondike trip beats the record. After a cold tempestuous journey down the Yukon, I reached Dawson City only to find a wildly exciting condition of affairs. Provisions were found to be running short in the town, and the expected steamboats did not arrive with relief. Three days ago the resulting panic reached its height among the 7000 people here.

I had been quick to perceive the trend of affairs, and, having brought only 150 pounds of provisions through from the coast, I lost no time in buying everything that I could before the traders' stores were closed to the public.

I was not a moment too soon.

The panic precipitated a rush for food, and the crash came. The traders, both of the A. C. Company and the N. A. T. and T. Company, announced that no more flour, beans, bacon, rice and dried fruit would be sold except to those Klondike miners who had placed advance orders with the cash during June, July and August of this year. This notification, cutting off nearly 4000 unprovided people, caused widespread consternation. Flour jumped in price from $6 a sack of 50 pounds to $100 a sack, and a few would sell to their neighbors even at this price. Bacon, beans, etc., all jumped to $1 a pound, and few sellers. Understand, this trading was outside of the stores among the people.

Today flour in Dawson City cannot be bought for $150 per sack of 50 pounds.

Hundreds are fleeing in boats down the Yukon amidst the floating ice, hoping to reach Fort Yukon, 320 miles distant, where there is a large stock of provisions, but not enough, I am afraid, for the multitude of unprovided persons. There will be terrible times in this country before the spring comes, and deaths from starvation will probably be numbered by the hundreds, if not by the thousands. The American government ought to take steps at once to send a winter relief expedition to Dawson, as fully four-fifths of the distressed people here are citizens of the United States, while one-fifth are from Canada.

Such an undertaking could be carried through successfully, taking only experienced miners from Juneau, Alaska, to carry provisions over the Dyea pass in early March 1898 and bringing the same down on the Yukon ice surface during the last days of March and the first days of April. Sleds would, of course, be used. This relief would come at the time when most sorely needed, as no provisions can come up the Yukon from the Bering Sea before July.

It will be practically impossible for many people to escape up the Yukon River on the ice this winter, as there is no dried salmon here or along the river for the dogs which draw the provision sleds through the fresh snow in early winter. Late in the winter (March) some men can draw their own sleds, but only those of great physical strength and not weakened by privations. Two-thirds of the destitute people in Dawson are not miners, are not inured to hardships and would surely perish if they were to attempt to leave the country this coming winter. They are trapped. I have carefully considered this whole subject, and can reach no other conclusions.

Dawson, N.W.T., October 12, 1897

It is expected that from 30 to 50 tons of gold will be dug by mine owners on the Klondike within the next six months! During the same period a multitude of wretched persons, stranded without provisions, will probably sicken and starve. Bread riots are almost a certainty and blood will be shed. Winter is here and there is not food enough to sustain the multitude. The men who are in possession of a six or eight months' supply of provisions will fight to prevent spoliation by the famished horde. God only knows what terrible events will happen in this country before the springtime comes! The individual stores of flour, bacon, rice, etc., are closely guarded day and night in cabins and caches. Twice already has the ready Winchester cracked on the streets in Dawson and bullets have pursued fleeing bread thieves. One poor wretch, shot through the lungs, now lies suffering at the hospital. Men of the mountains, men of iron nerve in Dawson, are frightened. The Specter of Starvation is peering over the golden hills of the new El Dorado. Panic reigns. Hundreds of men are fleeing in small boats down the Yukon, hoping to reach the cached food supplies at Circle City and Fort Yukon. Scores of others are preparing for a desperate winter journey 600 miles on the ice up the Yukon, in an endeavor to reach the seacoast at Juneau. Some will succeed and others perish on the way.

The prices asked for food are something frightful. Flour is held at $100 per sack, or $400 per barrel. Two sacks of 50 pounds each were sold today for $300—$3 per pound! There is little flour obtainable even at these prices on the street. Bacon, beans, rice, etc., are all held to be worth from $1 to $2 per pound, and any man who offers to sell at these figures is surrounded by a score of eager purchasers.

Hundreds have not a two weeks' supply of provisions. Money does not count. It is the poorest kind of trash in Dawson. One may walk the streets with a gold sack as big as a policeman's club while his stomach is gnawing with emptiness. Old-time friends do not invite each other in to dinner. Grub even for one meal is too valuable. If a caller comes to your cabin he excuses himself at mealtime, and the excuse in most cases is accepted. Nothing is talked of but the "grub question." "How's your flour?" is the current query as one man meets another. "Any beans to sell?" asks one stranger. "None," is the response. The only plentiful thing in Dawson is gold, and there is enough of it and to spare.

And strangely enough, while the food panic prevails in Dawson and extends out to the farthest points on the Klondike, the trading stores of the Alaska Commercial Company and of the North American Trading and Transportation Company are still selling flour at $6 per sack of 50 pounds, bacon at 50 cents per pound, rice at 30 cents, dried fruit at 30 cents and all other things in proportion! But the stores are not selling to everybody. Only a favored few of the miners who have had "winter orders" guaranteed in advance, and have made advance payments on the same, can secure the food.

The traders state in justification that they are in honor bound to fill the guaranteed orders, regardless of the hungry "new arrivals," and they are steadfastly ignoring the multitude clamoring for relief. The stores do not contain one-half enough food for all of the people who are without supplies and it simply becomes a question of who shall go hungry and starve.

The action of the traders, Captain Hansen of the A. C. Company, and Captain Healy, of the N. A. T. and T. Company, in provisioning the mine owners on their advance orders, has naturally raised a storm of condemnation among the new people who have arrived short, expecting to purchase supplies here, and all sorts of threats are made to loot the warehouses and run the traders out. There are but thirty members of the Mounted Police force in Dawson at present and these few men are hardly regarded as an effective check to lawless outbreaks. That there has been widespread apprehension of a raid on the warehouses of the trading companies is revealed by the extraordinary haste of the "winter order" men in getting their supplies away to caches and cabins and places of safety. For a week or more mining operations have been practically suspended on the Klondike, while the men were rushing to the stores for their provisions and packing the same away.

Three articles alone are sold to the general public by the Alaska Commercial Company's trader—sugar, tea and condensed soups. By a strange accident several thousand barrels of sugar reached Dawson instead of flour and there has been plenty for all. No one is refused 100 pounds of the stuff, if he wants it. Tea is also plentiful. If men could live on sugar alone, there would be no famine in Dawson. Hundreds of them have bought sugar heavily, not knowing what else to do. Frank Bedoe, an old miner with a squaw and family, residing near my cabin, came home last night with a keg of nails and a barrel of sugar. "There is my winter's outfit," he said with a grim smile. "It is all that I can get at the stores."

The Healy store (N. A. T. and T. Company) is not selling a pound of provisions to anyone except on "winter orders" and the front door is kept locked most of the time. The "winter order" customers are admitted by a guard stationed at the back door. A considerable stock of dry goods, clothing and hardware in both of the trading stores is for sale to the general public at prices about double those charged for the same goods in San Francisco. Blankets are sold at $15 to $25 for extra-large pairs, coats for $15 to $20, pantaloons for $8, blanket shirts for $6 and $7, thread for 25 cents per spool, frying pans for $2.50 and lamps for $7.50 each, etc.

I especially mention the lamps because I purchased one on a wild speculation. There had been a run on lamps at the A. C. Company store and there were only two left on the shelves. A clerk gave me the tip. "Those are the last two we have. If you want one, speak quick." I spoke and got the lamp. Two minutes later a dozen men had been refused lamps. Yet not one of us knew where the coal oil for the lamps was to be secured. There was a limited supply in the warehouses, but it was all held at $2 per gallon for "winter order" men and no amount of persuasion could induce these fellows to part with a drop. On the outside the public was clamoring for coal oil and candles at $20 a gallon for kerosene and $1 apiece for candles, and clamoring frantically at that. "Light" can hardly be had at any price and to add to the terrors of a starvation period, it will be a period of intense darkness as well. There are not enough candles in town to supply one-third of the people and out at the mines the condition of things is even worse. There candles are absolutely necessary for working in the "drifts," as well as in the cabins, and the shortage has produced genuine consternation. With the sun above the horizon only a few hours during December, January and February, life in the Klondike without candles or kerosene will be most unpleasant. The worst feature of the situation is found in the fact that no substitutes to furnish light can be found. There is little tallow to melt down into tapers and lard is scarce.

The saloonists and dance hall proprietors in Dawson are frantic over the lack of oil and are offering fabulous figures for the fluid to the lucky mine owners who have it on their winter orders. Some of the places will have to close for lack of light. Half of Dawson will sit in darkness this winter for lack even of candles. These precious articles, which are sold at the Dawson stores on winter orders for $9 per box of 120 candles and for $1.75 per box at the stores in Seattle, Washington, are held to be worth $100 per box by the unprovided public of Dawson, and many offers of $1 and even $1.50 per candle are made on the streets.

If by some happy chance I am able to secure a little kerosene for my lamp this winter in exchange for candles, I will arouse the envy of the whole east end of Dawson. If I do not get the oil, the presence of the lamp will be something of a home comfort after all. It is a pretty glass lamp, with a blue globe shade and brass feet and would cost a round silver dollar in Cincinnati.

It should not be breathed above a whisper that I have secured a big supply of candles—175 in all! None of my neighbors are so rich! I am saving my eyesight tonight in writing this article by using two candles, which stand in front of my empty lamp.

The fact of the matter is I braced trader Healy so strongly and so vividly pictured to him the needs of a newspaperman who wanted to shed light on the Klondike mines that he finally nerved himself to order a clerk to sell me 60 candles for $4.50! You may laugh at my earnestness, but if ever I blessed a man for a good deed I blessed Healy for that one.

With this auspicious start my luck grew with the days. A loyal friend from Seattle loaned me twelve more candles with an injunction to return them if I could and if not—why, burn 'em! Two days ago another man, an acquaintance of the Skagway trail, arrived on a small boat from up the Yukon and he let me have two dozen candles for $2! Just because I was a newspaperman and needed light. To cap the climax, last night a dear friend, a grand good man who had secured two whole boxes of candles from the A. C. store on his winter order, gave up one box to me at the store price! Ye Gods! I walked a mile in the descending gloom of an Arctic night, garnered that box of 120 candles under my right arm and marched hastily home with it. Now I have the 175 candles, which have not been burned, on a shelf just over my Winchester rifle and nobody gets those candles. They are worth, at $1.50 apiece, the sum of

$262.50, and to me they are intrinsically worth double that amount. Such things as candles and lamps are but trifles down in "the States," but up here in the Arctic darkness they are inestimable treasures. It is no joke to be without light.

The candle situation may be summarized as follows: The trading companies this year brought in candles for about 2000 people and kerosene for 200 more. Boats coming down the Yukon this summer with Klondike gold seekers usually brought a box of candles to every two men, just half enough for the long winter. The result is that fully half of the 6000 people are totally unprovided with light. Even now in October, darkness comes before seven o'clock in the evening. In December the period of daylight will only extend from 10 A.M. to 2 P.M. and it will be pitch dark by 3 P.M. How people without candles or kerosene are going to cook their meals and get about inside their cabins is a problem that nobody can solve. Hence the frantic demand for candles.

Another dismal feature of the present situation is the unsheltered condition of fully 2000 persons who are still living in tents, with no prospect of getting housed in cabins before the severe Arctic blasts arrive. Hundreds of them helplessly contemplate an attempt to live the winter out in their tents. Many are certain to freeze to death, not being provided with fur robes and blankets to withstand the terrible cold. The handful of Canadian officials here seem utterly unable to cope with the alarming situation. I suggested a few days ago to Customs Collector Davis that the trading companies should be requested to open their empty warehouses during the severe months of winter to the unsheltered multitude and that big stones should be placed in the warehouses and kept hot day and night to relieve the suffering. Davis was inclined to favor the idea and I think it may be adopted. If something is not done hundreds will be in imminent danger of freezing to death in their sleep. The thermometer goes down to 60 and 70 degrees below zero at times.

The panic which prevails in Dawson over the food question has taken on many strange aspects. Hundreds of men, insane in their thirst for gold, yet unprovided with food for the winter, have doggedly refused to leave this place and seek safety at Fort Yukon, where 900 tons of provisions have been dropped by the river steamboats unable to cross the sandbars there during the low water of the season just closed. Fort Yukon is 400 miles distant on the river and is downstream. The traders and the Canadian officials have pleaded in vain with the destitute gold hunters to go before the river closes and it becomes too late. Only about 500 have heeded the advice and departed. Over 1000 more should have gone, but they would not, hoping from day to day that the river steamboats would yet appear with supplies and that all would be well. Half a dozen rafts, which recently arrived from upriver with beef driven in over the mountains and slaughtered at Pelly River, have slightly eased up the situation, but only for the time being. The last three rafts, which arrived yesterday, brought 80 head of cattle and 800 sheep dressed.

This meat was partly the property of Jack Dalton, who traveled with me in the Talkeetna River country in 1890. Jack sold his beef today for $1.25 per pound, and it was eagerly taken at that price. A dressed steer will average at least 600 pounds, and the gross profit on each was about $750, or $60,000 for the lot of 80 head.

Such figures seem incredible and would be in any place except Dawson and the Klondike. Jack Dalton, who is an expert mountaineer, drove the 80 cattle in from Chilkat over a rocky trail, assisted by half a dozen men, and was less than three months on the way from the salt water to Dawson. Other men with cattle have accomplished the same feat this year.

Dawson, N.W.T., October 12, 1897

Those who have departed down the river by every known form of primitive conveyance may reach their destination before the river shall freeze up, but to make sure of doing it, they will have to be expeditious.

Ice forms nightly now along the bank and the darkness and cold are hastening down upon us.

The shortening of the day in this high latitude is very rapid at this season. Only three weeks ago we were at the autumnal equinox, when the days and nights were of equal length.

In the short space of three weeks the days have lost nearly an hour at each end. And now even the long twilight which follows the sunset is over before seven o'clock. From that hour till nearly 7 A.M. the cold, still night holds undisputed sway.

Then comes the beautiful, slow dawn, little by little brightening the sky and tinting the clouds in the southeast, heralding the stately approach of the King of Day. It is well on toward eight o'clock when his red forehead first appears above the horizon. He is in no haste to disclose his whole face, knowing that he has to climb the sky but a short way, and has till noon to do it.

The beauty of the Arctic night has won the hearts of all sojourners in these high latitudes. It has charm to subdue and captivate the roughest nature. It is part of that fascination that has called more than one Arctic explorer back from comfort and civilization again and again, to endure hardships and sufferings in this frozen zone.

I am not speaking of the occasional splendors of the Aurora Borealis, but of the unearthly, indescribable beauty of the ordinary Arctic night, with its long, slow twilights at each end.

But to appreciate and enjoy this charm of the Arctic night one must be warmly clad in furs that defy the intense cold, and must be able to turn at will from all the darkling beauty without to the hospitable interior of a well-warmed, well-lighted and well-provisioned cabin.

What these coming Arctic nights will be to the wretched tenters at Dawson I shrink from even contemplating. If they shall be able to get quarters in the vacant warehouses, as I suggested to Customs Collector Davis, they may be able to survive the winter; but the discomfort, the privation and the resultant disease and death must in any case be great.

93

The work of building cabins is going forward briskly, but the supply of timber suitable for that purpose is growing scanty in the immediate neighborhood of Dawson. As it was up at Lake Bennett, when I was there about six weeks ago, so here also, the biggest demand in the labor market is for woodsmen to cut timber for building and coarse wood for fuel. A man can make what in "the States" would be considered very good wages chopping timber for fuel. At present wood is selling at $18 per cord delivered, but it is agreed upon on all hands that so soon as the Arctic night shall have set in the price will go up to not less than $40.

Dawson, N.W.T., October 12, 1897

At Dawson, if one has in reasonable supply for all expectable needs, food, shelter, fuel, clothing and light, he is in opulent circumstances, whether his claim is panning out or not.

To be able to live in tolerable comfort through the terrific winter is the chief present concern of the Dawsonites. Fortune may be courted next season if one can keep alive and well till then. But at present all energies, especially of the newcomers, are enlisted in the struggle for existence. The terrible likelihood is that hundreds during the coming winter will fail in the struggle, and that instead of themselves digging for gold, somebody else will dig for them a grave.

But possibly two-thirds of the Klondikers here are so well provisioned against the winter's needs that they will pass the season in tolerable comfort. The necessities of life having thus been provided for, their next thought turns to the getting of news by letter from friends left behind or by newspaper from the outside world.

It was a great day in Dawson, therefore, when the Canadian authorities opened up the Dawson post office. It was the nearest approach to a general holiday that I have seen in Dawson.

Scarcely a claim or a digging anywhere within 20 miles but was represented in the great crowd of unkempt and shaggy men waiting for their mail.

The post office had 13,000 letters on hand to start business with. These letters had come by many hands over the mountains and down the Yukon. Some of them had been two months or more on the way, being able to move no faster than could be advanced the freight of their carriers.

A mail courier, traveling light, can make the distance between Juneau and Dawson in less than half the time required by an incoming miner, burdened with a half year's supply of provisions. Such a miner "totes" 100 pounds or so of his outfit four or five miles forward, and then returns for another load and another and another. The mail courier, on the contrary, pushes right ahead without ever retracing his steps, and thus the time is shortened from one-half to three-fourths.

It is a pleasure to know that in a little while mail communication will begin to be kept open by courier with such expedition and safety as may be possible over so difficult a route, one beset by so many hazards and subject to the severities of an Arctic winter.

The 13,000 letters with which the Dawson post office opened business a week ago Monday morning were the accumulation of weeks, as one party after another had arrived by raft from up the river.

When at last the window was opened, the men had formed in a long and jolly queue, waiting their turn at the window. Long before night the 13,000 letters had been distributed, except a handful or so, for which no claimants had appeared.

Next to a letter from home the most prized piece of reading matter is the latest newspaper, only a couple of months old. Such a paper, on the day of its arrival on some raft or scow or dugout, sells readily for $1.

But it is an aggravation to read it and reflect what great events may have occurred since, of which we are ignorant, and which we may have to wait weeks longer to get the news of. Cuba may be free, Hawaii annexed and Africa partitioned; any of the crowned heads of Europe may have died with a whole consequent recasting of European politics.

And then the possibilities of death, fire, flood, financial crash, riot, etc., in our own beloved land! Andrée may have come back with a section of the North Pole to authenticate his claims as a discoverer. What may not have happened? I tell you, to appreciate the luxury of a daily paper one should have sojourned for a winter in a place like Dawson, where necessarily news is two months or more after date.

The current price for postage here at present is $1 an ounce. This does not guarantee delivery, but only reasonable exertion to forward the letter to its destination, the sender taking all risks. Some correspondents have paid as high as $100 per letter for guaranteed delivery at the earliest moment possible.

October 15, 1897

Early this morning a large, curly-haired dog with a black-and-white face and an open countenance came to the door of my cabin and looked in for a moment as if to say, "Please, sir, give me a bite?" I hesitated for a moment and then deliberately proceeded to cut one-half pound of meat off of a sheep that had cost me $1.25 per pound. The dog instantly appropriated the piece of raw mutton thrown to him with such apparent gusto that I felt constrained to add to his enjoyment by contributing a quarter pound of stringy beef from my table, the meat being too tough almost to masticate.

You should have seen the expression of astonishment on that dog's face! "Well, here is a benevolent man at last!" he seemed to say, and without more ado he promptly camped in front of my open cabin door, with the evident intention of staying for the winter.

He did not offer to enter the cabin, but would occasionally raise his big head and snuff at the stove, as though inquiring, "Partner, when will the dinner be ready?" Poor fellow, I felt sorry for him.

Brought to the Klondike from a land of plenty by a master who had now no food to spare, the dog was nearly famished, and as he went pleading from door to door he met with many a curse and a kick.

I patted him gently on the head and he looked up in surprise. It was unexpected kindness. How quickly came the answering look of friendship and fealty from the dog's eyes. He was my devoted follower from that moment.

Since then I have met him on the streets in Dawson and have received instant recognition among the crowds of men. Fido never will forget, apparently, the meal that I gave him when he was hungry.

October 18, 1897

Attended the first Protestant church service ever held in Dawson City. It was conducted by the Reverend J. Hall Young, missionary of the Presbyterian Church, formerly of Wooster, Ohio, assisted by C. R. McEwen, medical missionary. Both men arrived on Sullivan's scows a week ago. The service was held at 11 A.M. in a log two-story structure on the main street which the missionary had engaged from the owner, Mr. Napoleon, promising to pay $800 rent. He had let the small rooms upstairs for $20 per month each. These rooms were of a comfortable size and rented readily.

In the church room on the lower floor pine or spruce blocks had been sawed off in foot lengths for seats. A few boards had been thrown across some of these blocks and constituted the first church pews. The missionary's pulpit was a four-foot section of a spruce tree beveled on the top at a pulpit angle. His seat and that of Dr. McEwen was a block of wood. An old iron stove, with a chimney pipe projecting through the window, furnished heat.

Rev. Young preached from the text "Take my yoke and follow me." He told his hearers that a yoke was not a burden, but was an appliance to help carry a heavy burden, and then aptly stated that the weary men who crossed the Skagway and Dyea trails lightened their burdens by using pack straps instead of carrying boxes in their hands. He announced that regular missionary work would be begun and asked the people to bring candles with them to evening service and then take the same away. He also spoke of rustling cordwood for the stove and of establishing a church Sabbath school and prayer meeting. The doctor was a medical missionary who would contribute his services free to those without money. The audience numbered about thirty-six men. No women. The missionary said it was the first service he had ever conducted where women were absent. Collection netted some money. One man I saw give $2.50. Another service is to be held tonight at 7 P.M.

October 22, 1897

Today I completed a painted sign, "Klondike City," to be hung out on the riverfront of the village where I live, which place has heretofore been called "Lousetown." Three of us in congress assembled a few days ago, decided that the name of the town should be changed. It was irrelevant and scurrilous, since the Indians who formerly resided here had moved in a body two miles down the Yukon, below Dawson City, and had built new domiciles.

The Lousetown of yesterday was the trim new Klondike City now and we proposed to have the world know the fact. Hence the sign.

O'Brien, the trader, rustled a neat spruce board, planed on both sides, and then secured a can of black paint. For my part I furnished a mucilage brush for lack of a better tool and then went at the job of sign painting, first drawing the outlines carefully with a lead pencil. The result was declared satisfactory by all of the onlookers in the store and it was unanimously decided to throw our banner to the breeze Saturday, when the paint would be dry.

Dawson City, the opposition town, lies just across the Klondike River and claims about 4000 citizens, more or less. Klondike City, alias Bugtown, contains many new cabins and boasts about 1000 inhabitants. In the days to come there will be rivalry between the two cities, something after the style of the St. Paul and Minneapolis fight. So far I have not heard from the Canadian authorities or the Mounted Police on our high-handed act in organizing a new city without the permission of Parliament.

October 23, 1897

There is no opening for a live daily newspaper in Dawson. The merchants would not advertise "slaughter sales" of their goods, at $1 per square. Nobody would advertise, except the real estate brokers and readers who wanted something to eat and were anxious to find somebody who would sell to them!

A paper might "go" if the subscribers would bring in cordwood and potatoes to pay up their arrears, but the difficulty is that they wouldn't do it. They would insist on paying money instead. No editor or publisher could stand such a racket as that in Dawson. He would freeze or starve to death, perhaps both. However, it is useless to consider the subject further. Nobody brought in type or a printing press.

This morning I managed to purchase some food from the Healy store. To speak strictly, I began preparations for the purchase last evening. At that time I handed a note to Healy's son requesting him to secure an answer for me today. The note requested the Captain to OK my order for 5 pounds of butter, 3 tin cans of evaporated cream and 10 pounds of bacon. The trader, who is spending most of the time at home to avoid the importunities of the hungry throngs, sent the note back with "OK Healy" written on it and when I entered the store several hours ago young Healy handed it to me. I presented the paper to a clerk and he, in turn, referred me to the general superintendent of the store, Mr. Chute, who carefully read the document, made me out an order on a printed blank for 2 rolls of butter at $1.25 a roll, 3 cans of evaporated cream at 50 cents a can and 12 pounds of bacon at 50 cents per pound. The order was then taken to the clerk and filled, I paying $10 cash for the provisions. There was 3½ pounds of butter in the two rolls taken together.

October 30, 1897

The "Yukon Chamber of Mining and Commerce," a small clique of *Examiner-Journal* people, Livernash, Meisner and Alex Mac-Donald, and Captain Hansen, organized behind barred doors in Captain Hansen's office—press all barred except Livernash and Edward Meisner. This "Chamber" called a public meeting today in the barroom of the Great Northern Hotel and posted notices of same about Dawson and up the gulch. There was an attendance of perhaps 300 men. The chairman was barkeeper Bill McFee. Livernash was the real presiding officer. He read a memorial to the Governor-General-in-Council of Canada, stating in well-put terms that the Yukon country could not afford to pay 20 percent royalty to the Crown and that the effect of the enforcement of this regulation would be to drive miners across to Alaska. Livernash urged that the Canadian authorities rescind this regulation and also the one giving every alternate claim of 100 feet to the Crown.

At the close of the reading of the document Livernash urged its adoption in a speech. He was followed by whiskey dealer Sullivan, who advised people to send the document by a committee to Ottawa.

McFee put a motion to adopt the memorial despite an amendment to have it read section by section and arbitrarily ruled out all opposition. The motion to adopt was carried by a moderate voice vote, many refusing, especially Canadians, to voice their wishes. Nearly two-thirds of the assemblage left the hall at once, in adjournment, although an invitation to sign the memorial at once was given to all. "Big advertisement for the *Examiner*" was the general verdict. Many Canadians present objected to the memorial unless another was sent to the U.S. Congress to repeal the Alien Labor Act.

November 2, 1897

This day was notable from the fact that I rustled some coal oil. Early in the morning Campbell said to me, "I will let you have a gallon of coal oil." So I secured the loan of the tinner's own oil can (glass and tin), holding a gallon. It stood outside of the door and was covered with the snow. When I got to the cabin I discovered that there was almost a pint of the coal oil in the bottom of the can. What a discovery! The bit of precious fluid, worth at current street prices nearly $2.50, was carefully transferred to my empty lamp and smeared over the cabin floor as well. Kerosene at $20 per gallon smells like perfume, don't you know? I lit the lamp this evening and it burned brilliantly. Such a light! I felt like going out and calling my neighbors in to see it, but then they would only have been envious and said something about "a bloated bondholder" or made other unpleasant remarks, so I desisted from my purpose.

As the lamp holds one quart of oil worth $5, you may well imagine that I shall only use it on state occasions—Thanksgiving, Christmas, New Year's, etc. What troubles me most is the anxious question as to whether I ought to return the half quart of oil to the tinsmith. Maybe he forgot the oil was in the can. I suspect he did forget. But, hold! He told me that I might have difficulty in getting the can away from the side door of his cabin—that his wife might chase me away. Now I know why he said it. He knew and his wife knew that the can contained that half quart of oil. I will not have to return the oil, but only the can!

Dawson, N.W.T., November 3, 1897

Beware of the Yukon "moose ranches"! Fully 1000 of them will be offered for sale within the next six months on the San Francisco and New York stock markets, provided conditions are favorable. The old time Western sport of snipe hunting with a bag is about to be improved upon by a new game, which will be tried on 10,000 "innocents" supposed to be anxious to make money quickly. These persons reside in the United States, Canada and Europe. They will be offered "moose ranches" at bargain rates, varying from $5,000 to $15,000 each, cash down, on delivery. Any moose found loitering upon the premises at the time of sale will be thrown in free of extra cost. All of the ranches in question are located upon the Klondike and Indian rivers.

In the mining camps of California, Colorado and Nevada, properties similar to the Yukon "moose ranches" have been known as "wildcats," and, well seasoned with "salt," have proved tempting morsels to the strangers from the East. Many of the speculators who profited by selling the "cats" among the Southern hills are now on the Yukon buying up ranches for a song. Within a few months numerous agents will leave Dawson City for "outside," taking with them certain deeds, bonds, etc., which is all of the paraphernalia needed to carry on their little games. You, austere reader, with a secret hankering for Klondike property, may be asked to "take a hand." But have a care! It is far better to buck the tiger in an out-and-out gambling game, where you have two chances out of five in your favor, than to invest in one of the "ranches," which will almost surely bring you no returns.

In plain English, the atmosphere of Dawson is impregnated with mining swindles. While a few good properties in the shape of "placer claims" are to be offered for sale in American and European mining markets, the intention of the speculators here is to enormously inflate the list of "claims" for sale with worthless strips of land along the Klondike and Indian rivers, both tributaries of the Yukon. The term "moose ranches" has been aptly applied to these holdings, as nothing except moose has ever been found upon them.

Reports reaching Dawson from outside, indicating that there was a fever of excitement over the Klondike, have spurred the speculators to prodigious activity. Options on claims, good, bad and indifferent—mostly indifferent—are being secured in large numbers. Many of the claims are "bonded" for sale in "the States." In numerous instances men arriving here have been given bonuses to stake claims along the Klondike at indicated points, the properties being immediately turned over to the speculators. In this way bunches of ten, twenty, fifty and one hundred claims have been secured by certain "operators" to sell to the lambs "back East." Such manipulations are possible under the existing Canadian mining regulations, which permit men to hold "claims" for nine months after staking and recording the same without doing any work on the ground. This interval is believed to be sufficiently long to enable the claim-holders to find purchasers in eastern Canada and the United States. It is not my intention to decry the Klondike, but merely to point out, as clearly as I can, the dangers which any reader of the Scripps-McRae newspapers will encounter in making a dash at Klondike mining properties offered for sale in Wall Street or elsewhere. It is always better to leap with one's eyes wide open, you know.

The El Dorado and Bonanza placers are located on branches of the Klondike and include the richest claims. Some portions of El Dorado gulch contain the largest placer gold deposits ever discovered in modern times—if not since the world began. It does not necessarily follow, however, that all portions of El Dorado and Bonanza are equally rich. In fact, the reverse is the case. There are "blanks" or "moose ranches" on both El Dorado and its companion gulch, if the latest "prospects" are to be relied upon. This is especially true of Bonanza. On the Klondike River itself not one

103

paying claim is yet in operation, although it is alleged that "prospects" are fair in one or two places. Nevertheless, the Klondike has been staked from its mouth clear up to Bonanza Creek, and "Klondike claims" will be upon the market before a single "drift hole" has been sunk to bedrock. Up to the present no one has found the bedrock on the lower Klondike. There may be gold lying upon it, but old miners are skeptical. No one, so far, has found it there. Prospect holes are to be sunk this winter on the Klondike.

The same things may be said of the mouth of Bonanza Creek, where it joins the Klondike. The entire area has been staked and recorded on the supposition that gold may be found there. Such discovery is possible, but old-timers in the country are not offering money for the ground, as they are doing for ground in other localities.

On Hunker Creek, another branch of the Klondike, good prospects have recently been found, and it is generally believed that there will be rich developments on certain Hunker claims, but not on all of them. Several other creeks along the Klondike show good prospects, but the demonstration of values has yet to be made.

To date nearly 2000 "claims" along the Klondike have been staked and recorded, of which 40, perhaps, have yielded enormously rich returns, and the others, so far as developed, from $50,000 down to one cent and less. There are numerous "one-centers."

Over the divide from the Klondike lies Indian River, and on two of its branches, Sulphur Creek and Dominion Creek, extraordinarily rich diggings have been struck. Sulphur, it is predicted, will rival El Dorado as a gold-producing spot, but as yet only a few claims are in operation there, owing to the difficulty of freighting over supplies.

One can find "moose ranches" on Sulphur and Dominion creeks as easily as he can on the Klondike. Every foot of Sulphur and Dominion is staked.

It is my intention, later on, to send back to the Scripps-McRae

newspapers for publication a shaded map of the Klondike and
Indian rivers on which will be indicated the best gold districts. Up
to the present time development has not proceeded sufficiently far
to allow of the making of a reliable map.

November 3, 1897

There is something new under the sun—at least under the Arctic
sun. A press club was organized here this evening which has all of
the literary hues of the Aurora Borealis. The leading newspapers of
the United States were represented at a meeting for organization,
in response to the following call, issued by an impromptu
committee:

Dawson, Oct. 26, 1897

Messrs. _____, Dear Sir:

Your presence is requested at an informal meeting of representatives of American newspapers to be held Wednesday evening, November 3rd, at the office of J. J. Rutledge, Main Street, Dawson City. It has
been suggested that an Arctic Press Association be formed, to the end
that a bond of good fellowship be established between the various correspondents, and that arrangements shall be made for a press dinner on
Thanksgiving or New Year's Day.

Furthermore, it is proposed to have a picture taken of the correspondents attired in winter costumes. Possibly the various newspapers represented would like to carry cuts showing the group of American newspaper men attired in Arctic furs and with the Aurora Borealis,
ice-bergs and snow-banks for a back-ground.

You are aware of the fact that at no time has there been such a
gathering of newspaper men in the polar regions of the earth.

These men are here to represent the leading journals of the
United States.

105

The idea is advanced for consideration that the first President and Secretary for the Association be chosen by lot.

> Sincerely yours,
>
> E. H. Wells
> Scripps-McRae League
>
> Omer Mearis
> Chicago *Record*
>
> B. A. Seitz
> Chicago *Record*
>
> Wm. J. Jones
> Post-Intelligencer Alaska News Syndicate

The following newspapers were directly represented at the meeting: New York *Tribune* by E. M. Hutchinson; New York *Journal* and San Francisco *Examiner* by E. N. Livernash; Pittsburgh *Post* by W. C. Wilkins; New York *World* and San Francisco *Call* by S. W. Wall; Seattle *Post-Intelligencer* and syndicate of other newspapers by Wm. J. Jones; Chicago *Record* by Omer Mearis; the Scripps-McRae League by yours truly. The New York *Herald* was off on a tramp up El Dorado Creek, but sent word by its representative, John McGilvery, that it wanted to be included in the organization.

Chappan Adney, of *Harper's Weekly,* who had just arrived from upriver amidst floating ice, sent similar word. A desperate effort had been made to find the fascinating Miss Kelly, correspondent of the Kansas City *Star,* who had also just reached Dawson, but the committee of bachelors were unable to locate her in time to issue an "invite." She will be asked later.

The New York *Times* was reported to have a representative in camp, E. LeRoy Pelletier, but he failed to materialize at the meeting. Artists Krelling of the *Examiner-Journal,* Mayberry of the New York *Herald* and Seitz of the Chicago *Record* were mysteriously absent, but were reported to be in tractable humor and ready to join the club. Another candidate was reported in the person of H. C. Kirk of the *Examiner-Journal* party.

While these correspondents primarily represented the newspapers mentioned, some of them supplied Klondike news to outside syndicates. It is fair to estimate the number of journals interested, directly and indirectly, at forty-five or fifty.

Despite the august character of the assemblage the committee on invitation had neglected to supply the necessary number of half-barrels for seats. Nobody was so impolite as to take ostensible notice of the fact, but the New York *Journal* inadvertently called attention to the matter by sitting down upon the floor, which, by the way, had a carpet on it. The Cincinnati *Post* also sat upon the floor as partial atonement for the omission. The New York *Tribune* curled up beside the one table and appeared satisfied. The other newspapers occupied seats.

The object of the meeting having been stated by your correspondent as temporary chairman, the call was read and it was decided to organize at once upon the lines proposed and to select the first President and Secretary by lot. Accordingly the names of the correspondents were written upon slips of paper and placed in a hat. The Chicago *Record* was given the privilege of drawing one slip from the hat, the man named thereon to be the President of the organization.

All of the newspapers held their breaths while the drawing was in progress. The New York *Journal* looked uneasily at the New York *World,* while the Cincinnati *Post* and the Pittsburgh *Post* gazed attentively into each other's eyes.

The slip contained the name of W. C. Wilkins. Pittsburgh had won! New York, San Francisco, Seattle and Cincinnati were out in the cold. But it didn't matter. We all felt glad for Wilkins.

Again the hat was filled with slips of paper for the purpose of choosing a Secretary, and the San Francisco *Call* was permitted the honor of drawing the name. The office fell to the Seattle *Post-Intelligencer.* Jones was the man.

No constitution was sprung upon the meeting for adoption, nor was any time limit placed upon the offices of President and Secretary. The newspapers present reserved the right to bounce the new officers on twenty minutes' notice if they refused to behave themselves.

It was unanimously decided to hold a Thanksgiving Day banquet, and a committee consisting of Livernash, Mearis and Wells was appointed to find a suitable place for the feast and to secure edibles for the table—no easy undertaking in a starvation camp. Hutchinson was chosen toastmaster.

The question of publishing a newspaper for the occasion was brought up and finally approved. The editorship was determined by drawing lots, and McGilvery captured the job. Every correspondent was asked to contribute an article for the paper, subject to the approval of the Editor. In default of a Hoe perfecting press, or one of Potter's double-deckers, it was decided to have only a limited edition printed on a typewriting machine, one copy for each of the correspondents. Had a Business Manager been created for the occasion, he would no doubt have kicked against the small edition and would have insisted upon printing an affidavit to 40,000 circulation, but the Editor was to be boss of this paper and a Business Manager was tabooed.

Before adjournment a committee was appointed to ascertain the whereabouts of the fair correspondent of the Kansas City *Star* and invite her to be present at the next meeting on Saturday night, when the committees will report.

The correspondents propose further to have a group photograph taken at noon on Thanksgiving Day. Livernash insists that he will appear in mid-summer costume if the other correspondents wear Arctic furs. We hardly know what to do with him.

Dawson, N.W.T., November 8, 1897

The Yukon River was closed by ice yesterday for the first time this year. Later in the day the jam broke and the heavy floes of three-foot ice continued to float rapidly past the town. At 4 P.M. a skiff loaded with provisions and manned by three Klondikers from Seattle came drifting downstream and was with difficulty landed through the assistance of men on shore. About 7 P.M. another boat carrying four Seattle men with their outfits was discerned in the gloom. Two of the voyageurs, taking a line, jumped overboard on the moving floes, and tried to land. One got safely to the bluff above Klondike City, while the other man fell into the water but managed to get out and reach the shore. The one on the edge of the perpendicular bluff was unable to advance or retreat and remained penned on his narrow perch until one o'clock this morning, when a rescuing party with ropes appeared on the top of the bluff and hauled the poor fellow up out of his perilous position.

In the meantime, the skiff with its two remaining passengers drifted down opposite Dawson, when the flow was suddenly checked by a jam, leaving the men in their frail bark several hundred feet from the bank. The ice was too treacherous to permit of crossing on it and, besides, the men did not care to desert the boat and provisions. All night they lay in the river surrounded by floes, in momentary expectation that their boat would be ground to pieces. At 3 A.M. the ice again began to move and a lead of open water appeared which enabled the two men to pole across to the shore ice, where ready hands assisted them in landing.

These men brought information of a skiff, heavily loaded with provisions, which they saw deserted upon the top of an ice jam twenty miles above Dawson. Whether the men who owned it perished will probably remain a mystery. There is little doubt that scores of boats caught in the ice jams above have been imperiled and wrecked with more or less loss of life. The great winter tragedy of the Yukon has begun! It is to be expected that several hundred men will lose their lives between Dawson City and the headwaters of the Yukon before the springtime comes.

Nearly 600 are preparing to leave here over "the first ice" for Juneau and the Pacific Coast. It will be good fortune, indeed, if half of these adventuresome persons get out alive. Few of them have any conception of the terrible rigors of an Arctic winter, or of the difficulties and dangers ahead. They are going "light," pulling their own hand sleds in many cases and usually with small quantities of provisions. To make the matter worse, not one half of the crowd are provided with sleeping sacks or fur robes, but are depending upon blankets to sleep in during nights when the temperature will fall 70 degrees below zero!

The majority are preparing to leave here with scant forty days' provisions, whereas the journey will, in most cases, surely require two months. There are no trading posts along the route where provisions can be obtained and few Indian villages. The men who run short of rations will be in a terrible plight, their only hope being that of securing food from chance travelers entering the country. This resource will avail in very few cases and the horrors of starvation will overshadow the trail. Before the March moon begins to wane, its pale light will glint upon scores of white, ghastly, upturned faces, half buried in the snow. This is no alarmist prediction. It is a certainty. Many men have met their doom in this country amidst the ice and snow of past winters and they were, as a rule, experienced and hardy individuals. My own prolonged winter trip through central Alaska in 1890–91 gave me an insight into the many difficulties and dangers of that sort of work, and I was well provided with sleds, dogs and furs.

No native-born Alaskan, or any old Yukon miner, would even think of undertaking the 600-mile winter journey over the ice from Dawson to Juneau without dogs to draw the sleds and fur robes for sleeping purposes. Yet a whole battalion of the newcomers are preparing for this very thing! In so far as I have had voice and influence both have been used to prevent this foolhardy undertaking. If men must make the trip I urge them to take along plenty of food and the necessary furs. In many cases it is advice thrown away.

While upon this topic it may be well to give some exact information regarding the outfits which men should bring with them into this country. No doubt there are thousands who are preparing for the trip.

In the first place, each man should purchase and bring through without fail the following supplies, which will last him for one year: flour, 10 50-pound sacks; salt, 20 pounds; bacon, well cured, 150 pounds; ham, 50 pounds; coffee, 20 pounds; tea, 15 pounds; sugar, 150 pounds; dried fruit, 200 pounds; rice, 100 pounds; butter, 100 pounds; lard, 60 pounds; oatmeal and other cereals, 100 pounds; 1 case (24 cans) condensed milk, weight 60 pounds; 2 cases corned beef, weight 112 pounds; 2 cases roast beef, weight 132 pounds; 2 cases beef tongue, weight 134 pounds; 2 cases canned tomatoes, weight 144 pounds; 2 cases canned cabbage, weight 128 pounds; 2 cases canned corn, weight 90 pounds; split peas, 50 pounds; 240 candles, 10 gallons coal oil in tin cases; 2 cases canned fruits; 1 quart condensed vinegar; 10 pounds evaporated onions; 50 pounds desiccated potatoes; 20 bars Ivory soap; 50 pounds pilot bread; 100 pounds black beans; 10 pounds baking powder; 2 pounds beef extract; 1 pound pepper; 1 pound mustard; matches in waterproof can, string, etc. Total weight of provisions—2785 pounds.

These goods should be placed under double coverings: first in light cotton sacks and then in heavy, oiled canvas sacks, to keep out water. Many a fine outfit has been spoiled because of neglect in this particular. If you cannot bring the provisions, etc., mentioned in this list, it will be far better and safer to stay at home, as the food supplies of the Yukon trading companies during the coming year (1898) will not begin to be sufficient for the army of people in this region.

In addition to the food it will be necessary to bring a sheet-iron stove for cooking and heating in a cabin, costing in Seattle $8; also heavy woolen underwear, a complete suit of gray mackintosh (waterproof), 3 pairs crackproof gum boots; 200 feet ⅝-inch manila boat rope; smaller sizes of ropes; medicines; canvas tarpaulin for covering goods in boat; carpenter's tools for raft building; gold pan, pick and shovel; whipsaw, crosscut saw, 2-inch auger for raft building; 10-by-12-foot A-frame tent; 2 rubber blankets; mosquito netting; pitch, 3 pounds; nails, 15 pounds; oakum, 3 pounds; 2 pulley blocks for hoisting logs; 2 Yale locks and staples; 1 fur robe, wolf preferred, 9 by 9 feet; 3 pairs heavy double blankets; 1 fur cap, 1 pair wool boots with Arctic overshoes, 3 pairs heavy German socks; cooking outfit, including only granite-ware pots of the best quality; Winchester .45-90 rifle, fishing tackle; 2 axes and a hatchet.

Heavy leather shoes are an absurdity. Three pairs of light hobnailed shoes are sufficient. Moccasins, obtainable in the country, must be worn during winter. Ordinary overcoats are useless. Two or three heavy shirts give better protection. It is well to have a dozen extra canvas sacks in the outfit for use in replacing torn sacks. A bolt of unbleached cotton cloth will be very useful. Folding canvas boats are occasionally of use, but are not strong enough for traveling on the Yukon. The sectional wooden boats sold by Seattle merchants are worse than useless, being positively dangerous.

Persons outfitting for a year's sojourn in the Yukon country cannot afford to take the advice of Portland or Seattle merchants concerning the supplies that are required. My observation has been that these gentlemen know little or nothing about the matter, although they will offer profuse information and even insist upon putting up outfits according to their ideas. Those who trusted to these men and came into the Yukon recently, have not yet ceased to bewail their ill luck. It is better, perhaps, to outfit in one's own town, attending personally to the minutest details, and then ship the stuff to the Pacific Coast. Some articles, however, especially Arctic woolens, cannot be purchased except at San Francisco, St. Paul or Puget Sound cities.

Having disposed of this question of outfit, let me offer one other bit of advice. Do not start out with the sole intention of reaching the Klondike. It is well enough to descend the Yukon and stop here for a few days, or weeks, if you wish, but understand that all of the Klondike and its tributaries are staked from source to mouth and there is no room for newcomers, except those prepared to purchase mines. Your plan of operations must be along the prospecting line. New streams may develop the wealth of the Klondike. There are hundreds of streams, both rivers and creeks, in Alaska and the British Northwest Territory.

Americans can well afford to prospect in Alaska, where immense quantities of gold exist, and where mining regulations are much more favorable than in the Canadian territory. Since the Canadians adopted the plan of allowing only 100 feet to a placer claim, instead of 500 feet, as formerly, and have determined to rob the claim owners of 20 percent of their gross profits, under the plea of exacting royalty, many Americans mining here have become disgusted and are preparing to try their luck in Uncle Sam's territory.

November 11, 1897

It was my privilege this evening to become a full-fledged member of the Yukon Order of Pioneers, an honor accorded to no other newspaperman in the camp.

The goat which I was obliged to ride was a wild one fresh from the mountains and of great strength and agility. Further than this I am not permitted to state, as the Order is a secret one. It embraces nearly all of the pioneers of the Yukon Valley, the Kentons and the Boones of the great Northwest who entered this region prior to 1892. They organized first at Forty Mile in December 1894, and limited the membership to those men who had been in the country prior to 1888. There were 25 members at this time. A simple regalia consisting of a shoulder throw was adopted, on which was

E. A. Hagg photograph of the Dawson City Chapter, Yukon Order of Pioneers, circa 1897. E. Hazard Wells is the second man in from the right, second row from the top.

inscribed the word "YOOP." No lodge building was erected, but a cabin rented for the purpose. Subsequently a branch lodge was instituted at Circle City, and Forty Mile was made the Grand Lodge. Soon afterwards the Grand Lodge was removed to Circle City, owing to the exodus of miners from the Forty Mile diggings. In 1896 the Order determined to admit to membership miners who appeared in the Yukon Valley in 1889. In 1897 the time was still further extended so as to include persons who came in 1890, 1891 and 1892. At present the line is drawn on 1892, and in all probability will not be changed again.

Jack McQuesten was the first President; Frank Dinsmore, Vice-President; Fred E. Hart, Secretary; and Bill McFee, Treasurer. The present officers of the Dawson Lodge are: Joe Cooper, President (Grand Lodge); Thomas O'Brien, President; H. Spencer, Vice-President; W. R. Lloyd, Secretary; and H. M. Smith, Treasurer. Dawson Lodge claims 60 members; Grand Lodge has 200 members under its jurisdiction.

The Dawson pioneers recently began the construction of a large log building, 35 by 50 feet in dimensions, which, when completed, will be one of the most substantial structures in town. It will cost $6000, and the lodge will use it for a meeting place, and occasionally rent it out for public entertainments, balls, etc.

Most of the members are gray-haired old men of the mountains whose lives have been replete with many thrilling episodes and strange adventures, and as the winter wears on I intend to sit with them about their cabin firesides and jot down the stories they tell me, one by one, to place before the readers of the Scripps-McRae newspapers.

Dawson, N.W.T., November 12, 1897

Splendor and misery are sadly combined in the Northwest Territory. I reside in a Klondike log cabin, 11 by 12 feet in dimensions, for which $650 spot cash has been offered the owner and refused. I get it rent free, although similar cabins all around me bring $50 per month from renters. When I offered to pay Bill Liggett, my landlord, for the use of this particular cabin, he snorted and said no. If I would take it on his terms—rent free—I could have it for the winter, but not otherwise.

Bill is an El Dorado King, you see, and an old-time friend. Together we tramped a few hundred miles across central Alaska in 1890.

My Klondike home has a glass window in it, with six small panes. It is valued at $25. Other pretentious residences nearby have no glass windows at all—the owners use unbleached muslin to strain the light through into their living rooms.

115

My house has a board floor. It hasn't been oiled yet, being new, but I suppose it will get oiled before the springtime comes. Ex-Collector of Customs Emmons, of Unalaska, has a cabin within a stone's throw. He has no floor at all, because the sawmill man wouldn't sell him one. Lumber gave out some time ago and there are lots of folks in Emmons' fix. I am sorry for Emmons. No matter how nicely he sweeps up there is always dirt around his stove and under the bed.

Coal-mine owner Risher, of Pittsburgh, Pennsylvania, occupies the cabin on one side of my dwelling. He is swelling around with a 30-foot-square cabin, but then he hasn't got it half furnished. In fact, he has curtained off one half of the interior with an old sail. He also has no floor.

Some days ago I purchased a dust pan. One of the neighbors kicked about it. He said it looked bad to see such an article hung up in a pioneer's cabin. Nevertheless, I use it and am not ashamed. In lieu of a broom, I am using a whisk brush to sweep up and it works nicely.

My stove is a sheet-iron affair purchased for $40 in Dawson and has an ingenious drum oven in the smoke pipe. I bake good bread in it, using flour worth $1.25 per pound, baking powder valued at $3 per pound and lard that holds its own in the Dawson City market at $1.25 per pound. A loaf of that bread is easily worth $2, perhaps $2.50. Don't laugh. I am making serious statements. This is the way we have things in Klondike.

My cabin writing table is a rare luxury. It is built of planed mill boards and is nailed firmly under the $25 window. The covering is bright red flannel, which cost $2.50. On this table stands a lamp which cost $7.50 and it is filled with coal oil. I have only a gallon of the oil to last me all winter, but that is more than any of my near neighbors have. I could sell it for $20—my gallon—but it is not for sale. I keep the lamp well filled and gaze on it frequently. It costs nothing to look at and it is so home-like. I intend to burn my lamp on Thanksgiving, Christmas and New Year's, and, perhaps, on the Fourth of July, if the gallon of oil holds out that long.

BILL LIGGETT, AN ELDORADO KING.

Cincinnati Post *artist's rendering of Bill Liggett from Wells's photograph. This illustration accompanied Wells's article on Liggett and his home on the Klondike.*

My chairs are two in number. One is merely a condensed soup box, on which I sit myself when there is company. The other is an easy chair, which I built and covered with canvas. A wealthy dentist from Peoria, Illinois, Dr. Van Sant, likes to come to my cabin and sit in this chair. He is fleshy and it makes him feel comfortable. Van Sant could cash a $10,000 check offhand in Tacoma or Seattle, but he has no means of getting a cabin floor or any easy chairs here.

My pine bedstead is not a beauty, to be sure, but I sleep never-

WELLS AT WORK IN HIS KLONDIKE CABIN.

Artist's conception of Wells at work writing in his cabin at Dawson.

theless under a fur robe that cost $150 in Dawson and blankets beneath that were purchased for $25 per pair. The equipment of the pine bedstead might properly be appraised at $250.

When I tumble out of bed in the morning, I put my feet into $2.50 socks and $5 moose-skin moccasins. I step across the bare floor to the $40 stove, strike a 5-cent match to dry wood worth $40 a cord and jump back into my $250 bed, because the cabin is cold. I rise after a bit, put $1 worth of tea on to steep in a $4 tin coffee pot, fry $2 worth of mutton chops and warm up $1 worth of flapjack bread. Then I spread a $1.50 strip of unbleached muslin upon the top of a $20 pine table, produce some $2-a-pound butter and $1.25 sugar and eat a comfortable $10 meal.

That's not all, either. I have some 75-cent ink and a 25-cent pen on my writing table and after eating I sit down and write a $7000 article on $1 paper sheets. Such is life in Dawson City. My illustrations may be homely, but they are true ones, nevertheless. Well may it be said that magnificence and misery go hand in hand on the Klondike.

One of my friends, an El Dorado King, has a cook of the genus female. She is a motherly, determined old lady who, with great courage, ventured into the Yukon country to make her fortune. And she is making it! She charges my friend William $100 per month and board for her services as cook. She eats $8 per day, Dawson City rates, or $240 worth of grub per month, making her total cost $340 per month! Isn't that pretty good for a cook? There are few of us who can afford such luxuries in the way of service.

But I weary of this recital. Money doesn't count for much in Dawson City. You may have pounds of the dust and be compelled to live on short rations. In fact, nobody seems to think of stealing gold dust in Dawson. A Chicago ham suspended overnight from the outside ridgepole of one's cabin will almost certainly disappear, but a sack of dust, in the same situation, would probably be overlooked.

Wells's photograph of his cabin at Dawson.

120

Wells's photograph of the cabin of his next-door neighbor, "ex-Collector of Customs Emmons, of Unalaska."

Wells's photograph of the Klondike River. Up to this point, no gold had been discovered on the left side of the river. However, every gulch on the right side contained gold in large quantities. According to the Cincinnati Post, *this was probably the first photograph ever taken of the Klondike River at this point.*

(From a Photograph Taken En Route.) *October 1899*

EXPLORER E. HAZARD WELLS,
THE POST'S BRILLIANT SPECIAL CORRESPONDENT WHO
HAS DOUBTLESS ARRIVED AT KLONDIKE.

Artist's conception of Wells in his fur "parkie."

123

November 12, 1897

Fred E. Hart, one of the oldest Yukon pioneers, was buried today. A cutting wind blew from the north and the thermometer registered 10 degrees below zero as the solemn cortege with the remains in a plain black coffin wound its way slowly up the snow-clad hillside back of Dawson. At length it reached a small opening amidst the whitened spruces where a grave had been excavated in the frozen moss and glacial ice.

The red sun of the Arctic gleamed coldly through the scraggy forest, lighting up the shivering forms of the mourners, thirty-odd of them, mostly elderly men wearing the badge of the Yukon Order of Pioneers and with gray hair, fast whitening under the blighting breath of recurring winters.

The hearse, which consisted of nothing more than an unpainted bobsled, drawn by one horse, had been dismissed and, at a signal from President Tom O'Brien, all heads were reverently bared as four strong men with ropes lowered the corpse to its last resting place. Then one by one the pioneers, picking up clods of the frozen moss, cast them upon the coffin. It was a solemn ceremony and unutterably sad.

No weeping mother, sister or wife was present to strew flowers upon the grave and to bathe it with her tears. The kindred of the deceased were far away in old Ireland, where two maiden sisters dwelt, all unconscious of the fact that their only brother was being laid away in the frozen earth. Only last year Hart went out to visit them, both his father and mother being dead.

Hart was 58 at the time of his death and had spent the best portion of his days searching in vain for the golden treasures of the earth. He had never made a stake, although one of the first men to enter the Yukon Valley. He came with trader Harper and another man from the Mackenzie by way of the Porcupine River in 1873, but soon after left the country, returning in 1887 and prospecting at intervals ever since. He reached Dawson in July 1897.

November 14, 1897

It is currently reported here that the noted frontiersman Jack Dalton was foully murdered several weeks ago on the Yukon River just above Rink Rapids. Men coming down from the Sixty Mile Post bring the story, which is to the effect that Dalton and his party of five men were held up by robbers, who, knowing Jack's fearless character and his quickness as a shot, took no risks but shot dead their victim and incidentally three of his companions, without a preliminary order to throw up hands. Dalton was accompanied on the trip by real estate dealer McGee and son, of San Francisco.

The money, some $20,000 in greenbacks and $(unknown) in gold dust, which Dalton carried, is supposed to have been the incentive to the attack.

Jack Dalton came to Alaska with me in 1890, as a member of the Frank Leslie expedition, and remained in the country, mining, prospecting and trading with the Indians.

November 15, 1897

Several parties of men left here today for Juneau and Seattle drawing hand sleds over the ice. I interrogated one party of five and found they had forty days' provisions each, allowing three pounds per day to the man. Their sleds were roughly hewed, without iron runners, and were heavily loaded. Each man drew his own sled.

It was reported this morning that the Palace Saloon had been robbed of $17,000 in gold dust by unknown persons, who carried

125

off three gold sacks. Among the losers was "Nigger Jim," a white man who recently sold his interest in Bonanza mining claims.

When the robbery of the Palace Saloon was reported to Nigger Jim this morning, he shrugged his shoulders and said, "Oh well, it leaves me just $8,500 less to spend, boys, that's all."

Dawson, N.W.T., November 16, 1897

The "society" of Dawson is truly cosmopolitan. A dance was held at "the Forks" by two restaurant ladies, the Misses Maloney,[3] inaugurating the social season among the Bonanza Kings. Most of the "straight" women in the camp were invited, but no "hooks." Tinhorn gamblers, bunco sharps and ex-convicts were strictly barred, so far as known. A number of saloonkeepers in good standing were among the guests. The affair was conducted with all possible éclat, an excellent supper being served despite the starvation panic. Several fiddles furnished excellent music.

It is hard to say whether more money was represented at the recent Bradley-Martin ball in New York City or at the Bonanza Kings hoedown on the Klondike of which I am writing. Millions of dollars were represented by men wearing blue shirts, jeans pantaloons and moose-skin moccasins, in place of evening dress suits and patent-leather shoes.

Among the celebrities present were Alex McDonald, Nigger Jim "and others," as the society newspaper reporters say. The total cost of the ball was somewhere in the neighborhood of $500, which bill several of the guests generously insisted upon defraying rather than allow it to fall upon the fair hostesses. The hat was passed for nuggets, at $50 a head, but when the two ladies who gave the ball were informed, they promptly forbade any further proceedings in

[3]The name of these two ladies has been variously reported as Mulrooney, Moulroney and Malone; however, I found three separate accounts of their activities in Dawson which give their name as Maloney, so that is what I have used here.

the matter. The Bonanza Kings who had already "chipped in" refused to take their gold back and an embarrassing situation followed, which was only relieved by the breaking up of the company, the Kings taking their ladies away and neglecting to pack off their nuggets.

Although the dance was given in a rough log building and with scant accommodations for onlookers, it was voted one of the most enjoyable events of the year.

November 16, 1897

An Illinois society lady sitting in a tent, with the thermometer 20 degrees below zero, buying and selling real estate, was on my visiting list this morning. She was richly attired in furs and tight-fitting gloves and wore a short dress of dark woolen cloth, beneath which peeped out a pair of shapely leggings, surmounting dainty boots. Perhaps this isn't an altogether lucid description from the standpoint of a fashion writer, but it is the best I can give.

It might be well to state that an aristocratic face, with firm chin and light blue eyes, appeared within the close-fitting fur hood.

"Allow me, Mrs. Keiser, to introduce Mr. Wells," said my sponsor, Mr. Christie, and thus Mrs. K. and I became acquainted.

"You see," she remarked, putting down her pen upon the little pine table behind which she sat, "it had been my intention for some years to visit the Yukon Valley. I had traveled extensively, but always felt that I would not be satisfied until I visited the great river of Alaska. When the Klondike excitement came up I saw my opportunity and at once publicly announced that I would accompany any gentleman and his wife who chose to take me down the Yukon. A married couple of St. Louis came promptly forward and we made traveling arrangements. My niece, Miss G. L. Osborne, decided to accompany me.

"We left our home in Jacksonville, Illinois, three months or so ago and with our friends started for Skagway. When we got to the Alaskan coast the gentleman and his wife backed out, but Miss O. and myself, knowing many people, soon found it convenient to continue our journey and finally joined Mr. Christie's party to Dawson. Of course, our departure on such a trip caused a sensation at home and the newspapers had a great deal to say. I believe they wanted our pictures.

"We are now here safe and sound and I rather like the town. It wasn't society, you see, that I came for, but novelty. Now that I am here it is not my intention to sit idly by. I am ready for business and propose to do some before the spring comes. I shall loan money on good security. Probably I shall secure some mining claims. At home I always managed my own affairs. Perhaps you know my brother-in-law, Captain John P. Keiser, of St. Louis? No? Well, of course our friends objected to the trip and all that, but we came and are not disappointed.

"Only one thing causes me regret. When we left folks told us to have our skirts cut short, as we were going into such a rough country and would get tangled up in long dresses. But we found there was no necessity for going about in kilts or short skirts and now I propose to have them lengthened. Miss Osborne is of the same mind. There is no need for women dressing in men's attire, as some claimed, in order to cross the mountains. Everyday clothing in the States is all sufficient on the Yukon."

Mrs. Keiser now turned to attend to a customer and the interview was ended. She resides in a log cabin just back of the Brewery Hotel. Miss Osborne is her housekeeping companion, and an attractive, vivacious girl. I very much fear that some of the Klondike money kings will be hopelessly smitten ere the Ides of March are heralded by Jack Frost.

November 18, 1897

The boom-e-ty, boom newspapers of New York and San Francisco are making desperate efforts to outdo each other in producing dismal noises upon the Yukon. A few months ago the San Francisco *Examiner* and New York *Journal* came waltzing along over the Skagway trail and were almost blown off the earth by the explosion of dynamite handled by the New York *World*. Pulitzer was advertising by blowing up thousands of tons of rock along the narrow causeway and the agents of Hearst were duly horrified. They corked up their ears and hurried past the baneful sound, speeding down the Yukon. Once in Dawson City the Hearst batteries were unlimbered and "ads" thundered into the sky to the great astonishment of the miners.

"All the poor and needy in the camp," said spokesman Livernash, "will be provided for at the expense of the *Examiner*. Mr. Hearst authorizes me to offer $50, or $500 or $5,000, any sum needed to relieve destitute persons here."

Bang! went the trombone and the bass drum together! Lawyer Livernash was soon upon the stump, calling upon the miners to assemble and protest against Canadian mining laws. Some came to the meetings. Then Livernash and Edward Meisner, of the *Examiner*, together with the post trader Captain Hansen and a wealthy miner named Alex McDonald, barred themselves in the Alaska Commercial Company's private office and prepared a petition to Canada to change the existing mining laws. A few days later a placard appeared upon the street announcing that a mass meeting of miners would be held to protest against the laws in question. It was signed the "Yukon Chamber of Mining and Commerce."

About 300 men attended the meeting in the barroom of the Great Northern Hotel, and the petition was read and signatures requested. Most of the Canadians present walked out without signing, while a few Americans put their names to the document. "Advertisement," remarked the majority, and smiled.

November 19, 1897

The plague of scurvy threatens to break out with great violence on the Klondike this winter. Insufficient provisions and the lack of a varied diet are the causes which are expected to lead to the trouble. By next spring it is believed that there will be fully 500 cases in camp. Fortunately there are thirty graduates of medicine here by actual count, and a fairly large stock of medicines, so that the disease ought easily to be ameliorated.

Dr. J. J. Chambers, physician at the Catholic Hospital in Dawson and a man of considerable medical ability, visited me and had the following comments to make:

"There were nearly forty mild cases of scurvy in Dawson last spring and I know already of numbers of men who have the preliminary symptoms—dullness, languor and slowness of motion. These persons will certainly develop scurvy within a few months. Then there are scores of men yet in good health who will soon be existing upon a few insufficient articles of diet, owing to their inability to secure a variety of food. These will succumb to scurvy by the time spring comes. I should not be surprised to find 500 cases in Dawson and the Klondike district.

"Another thing. I do not believe that the trouble results from eating salt pork. It is rather the outgrowth of eating too much of any one article, no matter what; existing upon that article, so to speak. The system gets out of order in consequence and the blood becomes thickened and vitiated. My observation teaches me that during the course of years men's bodies become accustomed to a variety of foods, each containing some particular substance, or property, needed for the proper nourishing of the system. A sudden change to a restricted diet at once causes complications.

"It is better, for instance, for a miner to bring into the country four kinds of dried fruit, say pears, apples, peaches and prunes, each of which has its special properties, than it is to bring all apples, or all prunes. After the present winter is over there will probably be enough provisions in the country to give every man a good variety and the scurvy will be stamped out."

"Is it a difficult disease to treat?"

"No, not if food of the proper kind can be obtained for the patient. It is not fatal, if taken under treatment in time."

"What are the prevailing disorders of the Klondike?"

"Kidney troubles and mountain, or typo-malaria, fever. There are nine cases of the latter now in the Catholic Hospital, some of them critical. The water of the Klondike and of the Yukon, for that matter, seems to possess chemical properties which act directly upon the kidneys as an irritant.

"Dysentery, in a mild form, afflicts 75 percent of the men landing in Dawson from up Yukon. Many pass blood from the bowels and bladder. In some instances the trouble is very difficult to check, although it usually yields to treatment in a few days. The Klondike water is worse, if anything, than the water of the Yukon.

"The way I account for the matter is this: Extensive forest fires burned off the timber upon the upper Klondike a year ago. The moss was also burned, exposing ice which had been covered up for ages, and which, thawing under the heat of the sun, set loose decayed vegetation which impregnated the water running into the stream."

Since Dr. Chambers accorded me this interview, he has himself been stricken down dangerously ill with bladder trouble, but is now slowly convalescing.

The Catholic Hospital is a commodious log structure in the northern part of town and is in charge of the Rev. Father Judge. He has no clerical assistant. Twenty-two patients are in the institution, which has a capacity of fifty. The hospital charge to patients is $5 per day, while the doctor's visits are each $5 extra. Any person residing in Dawson can, by an advance payment of three ounces of

131

gold annually, be assured of free hospital quarters in case of sickness.

As dentistry is somewhat allied, in its aches and pains, to the practice of medicine, it may be well to state, in concluding this writing, that there are four teeth-pulling artists in Dawson City, who charge $2.50 per jerk, balks not counted. An amalgam filling is inserted for $5.

Dawson, N.W.T., November 23, 1897

Ed Lord confessed to the first big robbery in Dawson. Small wonder, was it? Nigger Jim held a .48-caliber revolver to within six inches of the digestive apparatus which forms one of Edward's most valued accouterments and threatened to smash it into smithereens unless a theft of $17,000 was confessed and the cash restored to its owners—Nigger Jim and others. Lord weakened on the spot and without more ado led the way to the cache where the money was concealed.

It happened this way. A few days ago the Palace Saloon was burglarized and the cash drawer relieved of $17,000 in gold dust, which had been left on deposit by various individuals, James Doherty (Nigger Jim) being interested to the tune of $8,500; Jas. Cary, $5,500, and Lou Vernon, Dan Cathcut, George Gillan and M. Drummond for lesser amounts.

The robbery was a puzzle to the Dawson police authorities, but not to Nigger Jim. He suspected Ed Lord, the weak-minded barkeeper of the Palace, of knowing something about the affair. In fact, Edward, while intoxicated, gave a tip on himself to another man, and this person lost no time in notifying Jim.

Then followed a dramatic scene. Jim ran to his cabin, seized a revolver and sped away for the Palace, where he abruptly confronted the guilty barkeeper. "Hand over that money you stole!" shouted Jim, "or I'll slam you into hell in less'n half a minute!"

The barroom spectators, some half dozen in number, gazed with rapt attention upon the tableau, expecting every second to see Jim pull the trigger and Lord depart for below. But the latter desired to remain in Dawson and spoke up quickly. "I did it!" he exclaimed, "but Curley Judd, of Seattle, got me to do the job."

"Hand over the swag!" thundered Nigger Jim.

"It's under the A. C. sidewalk," blubbered Lord, now thoroughly frightened.

"Lead the way!" commanded Jim, and everybody filed out of the saloon and followed Lord up the principal street of Dawson to a point opposite the residence of the Alaska Commercial Company's trader, Captain Hansen.

"It's under here," said Lord, bending down and feeling under the sidewalk. A moment later he pulled out a heavy gold sack, then another and another, until the 1000 ounces of dust lay upon the boards.

Nigger Jim shouldered the stuff, while an opportune policeman marched Lord away to the barracks, where he will probably be imprisoned. Whether his accusation against Curley Judd can be substantiated remains to be seen.

Nigger Jim, the hero of the affair, is one of the whitest-skinned men who ever lived, his cognomen having been given him by the miners because he formerly lived in Louisiana.[4] He is a man of herculean proportions, always carries his nerve with him and is generous to a fault. He recently came into possession of $60,000 through the sale of his interest in a Bonanza mining claim. The next day he was seen upon the streets in Dawson, carrying a 100-pound gold sack upon his shoulder, announcing to "the boys" that he was paying his debts. In and out of saloons and stores he went, passing nuggets over the counters and wiping off slates. When Jim finished, late in the afternoon, he had still several pounds of dust in the sack and trudged wearily back to his cabin, being compelled to cart the stuff himself.

[4]As did the Mark Twain character from whom his nickname is derived.

CAPTAIN JOHN J. HEALY.

Captain John J. Healy (above) and Baby "Tot" Healy (right); both drawings from Wells's photographs.

Another interesting character, of an entirely different type, is Baby "Tot" Healy, granddaughter of Captain Healy, manager of the North American Trading and Transportation Company. The little lady, only 18 months old, was born in Circle City, Alaska, and is a prospective millionaire heiress, both her father, Tom C. Healy, and Grandfather Healy being heavily interested in valuable Klondike mining properties. In fact, the Healy family has skillfully contrived to purchase either whole or part interests in nearly thirty mining claims here, the value of which it is as yet impossible to compute. It is safe to say, however, that the properties will reach several mil-

134

lions in the aggregate. It is possible that they will produce ten or even twenty millions. The Healys are shrewd buyers, especially the Captain, who has been an Indian and frontier trader all of his life. He is now well along in his fifties.

His home, in the rear of the N.A.T. and T. store, is a modest one-story building of five rooms, carpeted and comfortable, but plainly furnished. The family circle consists of the Captain and his wife and daughter Alfreda; a son, Tom C. Healy, and his wife and baby

"TOT" HEALY,
Prospective Millionaire Heiress of
the Klondike.

daughter, "Tot"; O. W. Jackson, son-in-law of the Captain, and Mrs. Jackson, who is the Captain's oldest daughter.

Baby "Tot" Healy is one of those clever little people who always amuse, and she is usually on deck until 10 P.M., before being tucked away in bed. Her picture, which I include with this article, was taken several weeks ago, the tiny heiress posing gracefully out in the snow in front of her father's home. As yet she has only a vocabulary of half a dozen words, but makes up for the deficiency with many smiles. She will make her mark yet in New York society.

Miss Alfreda Healy, the Captain's 19-year-old daughter, owns a valuable Bonanza mining claim about nine miles up the gulch, on which she proposes to locate herself in company with one of her relatives. She will reside in a cabin, the same as other miners, and will superintend work on her claim. In this she will copy the example of her mother, who is a capable business woman, and who operates a number of mining claims, independent of any direction from her husband, Captain Healy. Miss Healy, who is by all odds the prettiest girl in the Yukon country, is well aware of her own prospects in life. A few days ago she said to me, "Indeed, when I go East within a few years, it will be under the guise of a poor girl. If the right man comes along then and wants me real bad, probably I will take him, knowing that it is not my money he is after."

Captain Healy himself is quite a noteworthy feature in Dawson. He never mingles in social affairs or in public meetings, preferring the quiet of his home. Yet the Captain is a strong character. He is the kind of man who makes enemies by a resolute determination to do as he pleases, and who does not care the snap of a finger because ill feeling results.

For thirty-odd years Captain Healy has been upon the frontier. Speaking more particularly of Alaska, he came to Juneau in 1885 and opened a store, but soon removed it to Dyea. In 1892 he had a chance to greatly better his condition. He had occasion to stop one day in Chicago, and there made a call upon an old friend, Portius B. Weare, a successful pork and grain speculator. From a casual conversation originated the rival company of Chicago capitalists—

Cudahy included—which has established posts at St. Michael, Fort Cudahy, Circle City and Dawson City.

Dawson, N.W.T., November 21, 1897

Fully 600 men are leaving Dawson on the ice, taking the winter trail up the Yukon to Juneau, on the Pacific Coast.

Most of them are drawing their own sleds and starting short of provisions. A few of the more lucky have dog trains and furs.

It is my conviction that fully 300 will perish of cold and starvation on the way out. They cannot drag their heavy loads over the rough ice and deep snow inside of three months, and their provisions will barely last forty days.

Many have no fur robes or moccasins, and must freeze.

Swift Water Bill and James Boiler, who carried out my dispatches on September 24, are in trouble. Swift Water Bill has frozen his feet near Pelly River. Jack Dalton, the noted frontiersman, who carried my dispatches from here on October 14, is reported murdered near Rink Rapids, on the Yukon River. Another special courier will leave here in four days, bearing the latest news to the Scripps-McRae newspapers.

This dispatch is sent in care of McKay's dog-team party, leaving today. It will go fast, barring accidents.

Cannot the governments of the United States and Canada at once send a relief party into the Yukon to succor Dawson and relieve the suffering and starvation along the winter trail? Help cannot be sent too soon.

Rumors of war between the United States and Spain reaching here are not confirmed.

The Presbyterian mission church, just opened by the Revs. Young and McEwen, burned this morning in Dawson, and twelve men who were in the building sleeping barely escaped with their lives. Their provisions and money all burned. Relief will be furnished them sufficient to start out of the country on the winter trail.

The missionaries saved most of their provisions, which were in another building. The fire is a great blow to the church workers, and no other building can probably be had this winter. It was the first fire in Dawson.

Local authorities issued a sweeping order closing the gambling houses in the Klondike district, but were only partially obeyed.

It is believed that Dawson crooks are preparing for a grand raid upon the Klondike next spring when the miners are making their clean-ups of gold.

Rich strikes are reported on Hunker Gulch; also on Dominion and Sulphur creeks. There are no particulars yet, and they may be exaggerations.

The Klondike will send out from 30 to 50 tons of gold next spring.

Famine prices for grub prevail in Dawson. All kinds of provisions will soon be $2 per pound. There are fully 5000 persons remaining here.

Furs and moccasins are very scarce. Robes are $200 each; fur caps, $20; cordwood, $40 a cord; and flour, $300 a barrel.

Dawson, N.W.T., November 28, 1897

Whence comes the Klondike gold? There are many theories. My own is that an extensive crater, near the "dome," 20 miles from Dawson, coughed up the yellow stuff at some far-distant period, and that glacial action subsequently distributed the metal over the localities where it is found. In support of this theory I would call attention to the fact that all of the gold-bearing gulches head in the "dome," of which the extinct crater is a part, and that no gold is found on the opposite side of the Klondike away from the crater.

138

The apostles of metallic precipitation will, of course, scout this idea; but I stick to it nevertheless. Gold is of igneous origin; came out of the bowels of the earth, and that's the end of it. Probably several of Old Nick's national banks blew up below when the Klondike eruption took place.

My sheet-iron cabin stove burns spruce with a fiery energy. One day the thermometer was 45 degrees below zero, and I was obliged to open the outside door several times to cool off.

The stove is a plain box, 36 inches long by 12 inches high and 12 inches wide. It is supported on four iron nails driven into two logs. The oven is located in a drum in the stovepipe, and does good baking. The spruce which it burns cost $40 per cord, delivered.

Dawson has fully thirty saloons, none of them licensed, but all "permitted" despite the law; two barbershops, which charge 50 cents for a shave and $1 for a haircut; one incipient public library, just forming; two big stores—the A. C. and the N.A.T. and T. companies; several smaller stores; one meat market, where beefsteaks retail at $4.50 each; two dance halls, for disreputable females and forgetful husbands away from their wives; two sawmills; an uncounted number of lawyers, brokers, etc.; two jewelry shops; three secondhand establishments; one blacksmith shop; one tin shop, earning $100 profit per day; one public hall (Pioneers); three missionaries and 235 gamblers.

Now you have it down fine.

Brussels carpet can be purchased at $3 per yard. Both company stores sell carpets and find a brisk demand. Put this in your pipe and smoke it. Dawsonites don't all live in hovels.

Whiskey is $40 per gallon at wholesale. Dawson saloonists give it considerable medical attention, "doctoring" it with vile ingredients and charging 50 cents per drink. They figure 100 drinks to the gallon, and $100 receipts from the same original gallon, so the quantity of dilution can easily be figured out.

A pleasant little man is my friend Bob Morgan, of Seattle. He was, however, disturbed one day. "I feel like kicking myself," he said. "I left a nice comfortable home and a good wife, spent $1700 to

139

get here with my nephew, and for what? To wheel freight in the A. C. warehouse in Dawson."

The dogs of Dawson and Klondike City really deserve a separate article. There are about 2000 of them of all kinds, colors and degrees of meanness. It takes a Yukon native cur to snarl and bite in the most approved wolfish fashion. Dogs from outside behave better. Yet all of these animals are held by their owners at fabulous prices. Any kind of a dog is worth $175 at present, and some are even purchased at $300 each, for winter teaming.

Dog food—fish, bacon, etc.—costs $1 per pound. Each dog eats three pounds a day, so it costs $3 per day to keep him.

There are half a dozen horses in Dawson, which haul winter bobsleds. The drivers charge $5 per hour. Hay comes from Stewart River by raft, and is expensive. It is said the horses do not pay.

Dawson gamblers are having an easy time. The Canadian authorities recently "suppressed" faro and roulette in the saloons. The proprietors of these places immediately erected partitions, so as to cut their bars off from the "clubrooms" in the rear, and installed the gamblers on the other side of the fence. Now it takes three or four more steps to reach the bar from the faro tables than it did when the town ran wide open.

The Dawson limit on gambling, either at poker, faro or roulette, is $25 and $50. No big plunges are allowed. Several banks were hit hard on different occasions and were reported to be in tight quarters. Thousands of dollars changed hands overnight.

There are perhaps 30 women engaged in sewing in Dawson during the present winter. This number includes a number of squaws. The average earnings of each woman from sewing moccasins, doing mending, etc., are $1.50 per hour. They all have abundance of work. The 6000 men in the town and vicinity could give work to several hundreds more manipulators of the needle. It is not to be inferred, however, from the foregoing statement, that there are only about 30 women in Dawson. On the contrary, there are at least 200 in the place, of whom perhaps 40 or 50 are married, and the remainder single. There are quite a number of dance-hall girls in the town, mostly employed at the opera house. The charge made for a dance is $1, and the business seems to prosper.

Dawson, N.W.T., November 30, 1897

There is an El Dorado King snoring peacefully within six feet of me. He occupies the far side of my cabin bed, from which I have just arisen and, for aught I know, he is dreaming of steam yachts, Delmonico suppers and gifts to orphan asylums. His breath comes and goes in those easy, well-modulated cadences which bespeak the contented spirit. He was out late last night according to the fashion of El Dorado nabobs, and proposes evidently to make up for lost sleep this morning. I shall let him alone until the gray light breaks over the Yukon hills, and then he must get up.

My friend Bill Liggett,[5] the unconscious object of these remarks, is a six-footer from Holly Grove, Upshur County, West Virginia. He entered the world under somewhat discouraging circumstances in the year 1860. His father was by no means a wealthy man, owning a small farm, and Bill, together with his six brothers, began early to rustle for a living. Most of the boys drifted west, the sleeping subject of this discourse included, and entered various pursuits.

Bill tried farming, but the hot blasts of Kansas and the paucity of the rain supply made it impracticable for him to get married, and so he drifted north, using the Polar Star as his guide to fortune. In the spring of 1889 he entered the Yukon country, boating down to Forty Mile Creek, where I found him working on a claim a few months later.

In the summer of 1890 I again visited Forty Mile and discovered Liggett sluicing an unprofitable gulch claim. He accepted an offer from me to pack 100 pounds of provisions across the Tanana River at $15 per day wages, and thus became a member of the Leslie expedition. There was something about Liggett's grit that struck me most favorably, and after we had parted company through the

[5]For a sketch of Liggett, see page 117.

expiration of our agreement I always kept him in mind. His determination to win a fortune out of the Northlands was the most patent characteristic of the man, and grimly he stuck by his job.

After I left Alaska, Liggett kept on mining, showing considerable judgment in selecting profitable ground. Twice he made small strikes on Miller Creek and Birch Creek, taking out a few thousand dollars in surplus cash each time, which he carried back to West Virginia and "salted down" in farm mortgages, returning to the Yukon.

The subject of this sketch, as the professional biographers say, did not come to Klondike with the first rush, although nearby at other diggings. He discredited the fabulous stories that floated upon the winds from camp to camp and stuck to his job of sluicing some moderately good ground. But finally the reports came too thick and fast to be doubted longer and Bill made an offhand decision. Dropping his pick where he had been working, he rushed into his cabin, seized a few necessary articles of food and apparel and bolted down the gulch for the Yukon, leaving behind all his other property, mining claim, cabin, cooking utensils, tools, rifle and a big stock of provisions, none of which he has seen again to this day. Jumping into a skiff, he rowed furiously down the river, arriving in Dawson in April 1897. He quickly legged it out to the gulch and began surveying the ground. Other people had been before him in staking off the best territory, and Bill's chances were slim. But he was not to be downed easily. Casting his experienced eye over El Dorado Creek, a branch of the Klondike, he decided to make or break by the biggest gamble of his life.

Turning to the owners of claim No. 13, and scouting the unlucky number, he boldly offered $31,250 for a three-eighths interest in the 500-foot strip of ground. The offer, which seemed to be a phenomenally large one, was eagerly snapped up, and Bill found himself installed in three-eighths possession, with Messrs. Chute owning one-eighth, Gates two-eighths, Mallory one-eighth and Turner one-eighth. As Bill had loaned out all of his ready money, and was only worth, at best, $10,000, he was obliged to run in debt for his entire interest, promising to pay from the proceeds of the claim when he struck bedrock. His partners considered him the best man to operate the claim, and put everything into his hands as super-intendent at $20 per day.

And now Bill did some of the finest rustling of his life. Having only sixty days in which to pay for his interest, he rushed work night and day, laboring in the drift hole with employees and shov-eling out pay dirt with frantic energy. "I never sweat so hard in my life before," remarked Bill one day to me. "That $31,250 was hanging over my head and I knew if the money wasn't paid on the minute when due I would lose my interest, as the ground showed up so much richer than the late owner had expected. How we dug and sluiced! Great Scott, but the dirt was rich! I could hardly believe my eyes; nothing like it was ever known before! Well, we got the $30,000 out on time, all right, and I made my payment. That's how I got in on the El Dorado."

As Liggett's claim is one of the finest in the entire region, I will describe it more particularly. It is 500 feet in length, and extends from the base of the hill on one side of the creek to the base of the opposite hill—a distance of perhaps 600 feet.

It is not the width of the claim which counts, however, as the pay streak runs lengthwise through the ground. This streak is the most wonderful ever discovered since placer mining began. It has a width of from 90 to 100 feet, is from two and one-half to three and one-half feet in thickness and contains a ribbon of pure gold, about twelve inches wide and one-quarter to one-third inch thick, running through the deposit from one end of the claim to the other end. Prospect holes sunk at various points reveal a remarkable uni-formity in the ribbon and pay streak. The immense mass of gravel, averaging nearly 300 cubic feet to the linear foot, or 150,000 cubic feet on the entire claim, is studded with nuggets like plums in a pudding, besides bearing vast quantities of coarse gold dust. So far the claim has yielded $150,000, an average of $2000 per linear foot, as only 70 feet has been worked out of the 500. There are no "pockets." The largest nugget taken out weighed $105,

143

while the largest selected pan of dirt yielded $405. Pans of $100 and $150 are a common thing. Liggett pays off his twelve men every Saturday during the winter by panning a bushel of dirt beside his cabin stove, and wages are $12.50 per day.

If the claim continues to yield $2000 to the foot, as there is every reason to expect, the entire 500 feet will produce a cool $1,000,000.

This is no dream. I have seen the gold and pay streaks, and know whereof I speak.

And this claim, No. 13, was recorded in Dawson September 29, 1896, by unlucky Joe Hollingshead, who sold a one-half interest in it for $1000 and got rid of the balance before the big find was made.

Another striking feature of affairs is the intention of my friend Liggett. He wants to get out of the country next summer, sure pop, and proposes to mine what gold he can this winter and then sell his interest in the unworked portion of the claim for what it will bring—say, $100,000.

"I've had enough of this country," remarked Bill to me, "and I want to leave next summer sure. Eight years in the Yukon is a big chunk out of a man's life. If I wanted to stay here I could make piles and piles of money. But what would I do with it all? I couldn't spend it. No, I will sell out and go to the States. Probably I shall never marry. My disposition is too wandersome. I shall go to the tropics and try mining there. My strength is not what it used to be. The climate here is breaking me down. I feel it."

When I reached Dawson, Liggett insisted upon my taking his town house for the winter. Now he spends days here with me, and I, in turn, make his El Dorado cabin my stopping place when up the gulch.

Dawson, N.W.T., December 7, 1897

Many years ago, it is said, the French modistes introduced into the United States a fashion which provided that wolves should wear sheep's clothing. The American wolves took eagerly to the idea, and in large measure adopted it as the vesture of their kind. Up here in the British Northwest, however, the wolves do nothing of the sort. They are only too glad to appear in their own warm gray suits of fur and never offer to trade their garments to the mountain sheep for fluffy white pantalettes of curly wool.

The Yukon wolves' clothing is anxiously sought after by Klondikers who want to be comfortable at night. Ten big wolf pelts, sewed together, make one of the finest sleeping robes that can be secured. Such articles are very scarce in Dawson this year. A wolf-skin robe sells readily for $150 to $250.

When I came to this country I brought in some sheep's clothing, tanned, with the wool on, to use for sleeping purposes. In fact, I had a sheep-skin sleeping sack. It was but a makeshift at best, with a chilly "feel" on frosty nights, and I gladly accepted the loan of a wolf-skin robe from an El Dorado King. Now, I roll up every night in it and defy the cold that freezes things solidly in my cabin.

As a bit of advice to those intending to come here, let me suggest the propriety of bringing fur sleeping robes from "the States." It is cheaper to do so, and, in view of the scarcity of robes in the Yukon country, is a most prudent procedure.

The two big fur companies—A. C. and N. A. T. and T.—do not want to sell peltries in Alaska or the British Northwest. On the contrary, their upriver agents have strict orders not to sell a skin to anyone, but to ship everything to the central station at St. Michael, Alaska, where the furs are sorted over carefully and the best laid aside for shipment to the United States and Europe. The poor "summer skins" and others of a defective kind are then returned to the various posts for sale to the miners for sleeping robes. Hence it pays to invest in furs before coming to the Yukon.

An amusing incident happened this morning which vividly illus-trates the incongruous conditions prevailing in Dawson. Captain Healy, of the North American Transportation and Trading Com-pany, let me have two gallons of coal oil at the regular store price, $1.50 per gallon. This was a special dispensation, oil being very scarce and only obtainable by the exercise of the most exhaustive "pulls." My receptacle for the oil was a new twelve-quart tin pail which I had purchased of the Dawson City tinsmith for $3.50.

Presenting a written order from General Manager Healy to Local Manager Chute, of the Transportation Company's store, for the two gallons of oil, I secured the fluid in my pail and started carefully down the street, fearing that I might slip and spill some of it. I had not proceeded 200 yards when a secondhand dealer in provisions, etc., caught on to my pail full of oil and wanted to give me $30 for it! He said that he had a customer to whom he could sell it at once for $40—$20 per gallon!

My oil was not for sale, however, and the dealer went his way, disappointed. I am burning a few thimblefuls of the oil to write this dispatch. The sun does not show himself at all above the Klon-dike hills at present, although his rays gild the mountain peaks about noon. Still, there is considerable gray daylight, extending from 9:30 A.M. to about 2:30 P.M. The twilight is long-drawn-out, deep darkness not falling upon the valley before 4:30 P.M.

A few days ago, with a bright, clear sky, the thermometer took a drop to 59 degrees below zero. It kept its spirits down until a snowstorm arrived, when with a sudden bound it leaped to 30 above zero, and stood gazing down upon the Yukon from that dizzy altitude. Since the snow ceased falling the sky has remained cloudy and the thermometer keeps its neck stretched like a Canada goose. One now goes about comfortably with nose and ears exposed.

It is a peculiarity of the Yukon that a cloudy day, even in January, brings immediately a warm spell of weather, which endures only so long as the clouds hover overhead. The moment the blue sky appears, Jack Frost settles down to work again. Sometimes the temperature will drop to 70 degrees below zero, but only for a few days.

It gives one that queer kind of feeling to ramble along in the dust between whole rows of national banks and be uncertain which one to loot! Nobody is going to kick if you do loot one here, so long as you pay for the privilege. Each of these big Klondike hills is a national bank in itself and the government is perfectly willing to let any man help himself to its gold deposits, provided he pays his $15 entry fee to the local Gold Commissioner.

It is easy enough to pay the $15. Any fellow in the camp can make that much sawing wood in one day. But when he has paid the $15 to the Canadian Commissioner and has braced manfully up to his selected hill to take out a fortune, the troublesome question arises as to where he shall begin the attack. Where can he sink a shaft to strike the paystreak? There are thousands of acres of mountains, but not thousands of years' time in which to systematically perforate the big mounds where the financiers of the Silurian age buried their cash. It is possible to sink half a dozen shafts in one winter, if a man works hard, but the chances are ten to one that the paystreak will exclaim triumphantly, "He never touched me!" Burning for gold is one of the strange sights of the Klondike. As I passed up El Dorado Creek a few mornings ago, the still gray light of the southeast appeared as a background for numerous pillars of blue smoke jutting like Corinthian columns from the snow-robed earth to the heavens above. Flames seethed and crackled in the bowels of the earth, throwing occasional darts of lurid red upon the white-shrouded spruces of the forest.

Sometimes I would stop at the small craters of these miniature volcanoes and peer inside, only to be repelled by the rising smoke. Yet I knew that 20 or 30 feet below, the firewood placed by the miners had been burning all night, gradually thawing the frozen soil, so that the golden nuggets could be shoveled out.

Burning is slow work. Each fire thaws from 7 to 15 inches of the

147

Miners prospecting near Dawson.

148

A typical Gold Rush mining camp near Dawson.

149

surrounding soil, which must then be removed, and another fire kindled to thaw more soil. Most prospecting is done by sinking vertical holes in the valley to the ancient bedrock. The average depth of the muck and gravel above the pay streak is 20 feet or more. Once a hole is down on "pay" the miner builds his fires so as to drift along the streak of gold, sometimes going from 50 to 100 feet. There is no danger of winter cave-ins, the frozen soil being as firm as adamant.

Coming down El Dorado Creek in the deep gloom of early morning, I saw numerous phantom shapes in black moving slowly backward and forward, with their arms rising and falling in rotary motion. These shapes soon resolved themselves into men, hoisting pay dirt from the shafts with windlasses. All about them was a waste of Arctic snow and a cold, cheerless prospect. But the bucketfuls of earth which they hoisted were sodden with gold dust and nuggets, and they labored cheerfully on from early morn till late at night. Visions of stately mansions, steam yachts and liveried coachmen—visions, I dare say, of a Bradley-Martin dinner—floated before the eyes of some of these men as they strained and tugged at the windlasses.

Dawson City, Dec. 11, 1897

To telegraph operator at any station in British Columbia or the United States:

Wire following dispatch at once to Cincinnati *Post,* Cincinnati, Ohio, U.S.A., at the regular press rates, collecting tolls from Cincinnati *Post.* Do not allow any other newspaper reporter to see this dispatch and oblige.

Yours truly,

E. H. Wells
Klondike Correspondent
Cincinnati *Post*

ON THE KLONDIKE

TO: Cincinnati *Post*
Cincinnati, Ohio, U.S.A.

Dawson, N.W.T., December 11, 1897

Startling news reaches here from Fort Yukon, 400 miles distant down the river. Two couriers, Philip Lann and Fred Gasch, arrived bringing United States government dispatches of utmost importance to be forwarded to Washington by special messenger. These dispatches are bulky and relate to thrilling events at Fort Yukon and starvation panic.

Philip Lann, one of the couriers, said, "Captain P. H. Ray, of the 8th United States Infantry, heroically placed the Stars and Stripes above the two provisions caches of the Alaska Commercial Company and the North American Trading and Transportation Company at Fort Yukon, and donning his full uniform, as a United States officer, dared a big mob of men to attack the provisions or fire on the United States flag. He awed the mob into submission and is now dictator at Fort Yukon, which he has placed under martial law until next spring. Ray has no soldiers nearer than St. Michael, 1000 miles away, his only military companion being Lieutenant Richardson. The Captain is 55 years of age, a tall, commanding man and grit all through. He was determined not to let the mob of several hundred steal all of the provisions at Fort Yukon and leave other hundreds to starve to death. Ray has posted notices on both provisions caches to the effect that Uncle Sam controls the grub and warning all to keep hands off.

"He issues ten days' rations free to those without money, telling them they can get no more unless they cut cordwood for the United States government at Fort Yukon at $5 per cord, their pay to be applied on grub. Ray now has twenty-five volunteers at his back to enforce his authority.

"The Alaska Commercial Company's cache of provisions is in a frame building five miles down the Yukon River from Fort Yukon, while the North American Trading and Transportation Company's cache is in a log building at the station. The rioters have directed their attention to the Alaska Commercial Company's cache mainly. There are many men fleeing from Fort Yukon downriver on ice toward Dawson and there will be 500 coming before March."

151

Dawson is out of provisions for newcomers and God only knows what will be done with these fugitives!

There are 1000 white persons at Circle City and Fort Yukon, while there is scarcely 300 tons of provisions in sight and many hundreds of native Alaskans out of food.

There are 200 cabins at Fort Yukon and about 200 more at the Alaska Commercial Company's cache five miles away.

Harry Davis is the Fort Yukon agent for the A. C. C., and John Boggs agent for the N. A. T. and T.

The lower Yukon River is reported thronged by 2000 Klondikers and provisions there are scarce as well.

Captain Healy, general manager of the North American Trading and Transportation Company at Dawson, is much agitated over the latest news. He said to me, "We must act quickly, or there will be terrible times on the Yukon next year. The United States government must take steps at once to place all of Alaska under martial law and send plenty of troops to enforce order. Otherwise the two trading companies may be driven from the country and there will be no supplies for anyone. Use all of your power in the press to call public attention to this matter at once."

Captain Healy handed me the following modest letter from Captain Ray, in which the latter speaks but little of his heroic achievements. It is official and I quote as follows verbatim:

Fort Yukon, Alaska, October 30, 1897

Captain J. J. Healy
Dawson, N.W.T.

My Dear Sir:

I send Mr. Gasch with dispatches and he will explain the situation here more fully than I can write. I hope that Captain Hansen and yourself will take immediate steps to check the exodus down the river as far as possible. There seems to be some misunderstanding in regard to the amount of subsistence stores in the two caches at this point. Miners state that they were informed by Captain Hansen and yourself that the two companies had over 1000 tons, but I find in fact that there is less than 300 tons in the aggregate in both caches. This will feed about 1000 men until June 1st. There are over 300 people now here, Circle City is very short and I am reliably informed that there are over 500 people coming this way between Dawson and this place. Of course I will push as many on to Fort Hamlin as possible.

It is also possible that the caches here may be destroyed. Yesterday it came to my knowledge that between 75 and 100 men, calling themselves miners, had organized an attack on the A. C. Co.'s cache. I went up at once with Lieutenant Richardson and a committee called upon me and stated that as yourself and Captain Hansen had promised at Dawson that they should be allowed to purchase supplies here on credit and they demanded a year's outfit be furnished them. If this was not done before 10 o'clock the next day they would take it by force. As Mr. Davis did not feel that he could comply with their request, he refused. I explained to them that I would issue rations to all destitute and they went away. Lieutenant Richardson went over to their camp and they passed a resolution in his presence to attack the cache the next morning. Word was sent down to me. I at once posted a proclamation taking charge of both caches in the name of the United States, and the next morning I went over with about 25 men unarmed.

When within ½ mile of the cache I was met by one man, who said he was delegated to have me come to their camp for consultation, which I refused to do. He then came out in his true colors and said he would not allow me to go to the cache. As I did not stop he then asked me if I would wait where I was until they could consult, saying they had the cache. As I knew Lieutenant Richardson was in the building and there had been no firing I was convinced he was lying. I told him again that the stores were the property of the United States, that I would feed the destitute, give bona fide prospectors sufficient on their notes to go out, and defied them to fire, or touch the cache.

He went to the camp and in about 20 minutes returned with word that they accepted my terms.

I found Lieutenant Richardson in full possession and no attempt had been made to force the guard, though they had tried to get Lieutenant Richardson into their camp with a view of holding him as a hostage in event I should attack them.

As matters now stand I am feeding all destitutes on their oath that they are such. All those having money must pay for what they get. No man shall be allowed to purchase more than one hundred and fifty dollars' worth for an outfit for the balance of the year, and leave the place at once. All stores issued on my orders to be charged to the United States, your employees and business to go on as usual.

I believe the caches are now safe as long as I am in charge. This was not a case of starving men, but of premeditated robbery. If you wish to preserve your property, use your influence to have the necessary legislation so that troops, when they arrive next spring, can act promptly and unhampered. I urge immediate action through your friends in the States.

I have advised Captain Hansen that I have written you. Will you please show him this letter, and you are at liberty to use the information as you see fit for the public good.

> Very Truly Yours
> In Haste,
>
> P. H. Ray, Captain
> 8th U.S. Infantry

Another distressing feature of the situation at Dawson now is complete destitution of neighboring native Alaskans. There are three or four hundred in number who are almost entirely out of provisions.

> E. Hazard Wells
> Klondike

Dawson, N.W.T., December 15, 1897

When I reach home again one project shall surely be carried out! There is a corner drugstore near my house and they sell lamps there. I shall order six lamps at once, have them filled with 12-cent coal oil by the grocer's boy and then put the whole half dozen hard at work furiously shedding light for my personal benefit. It

Wells's "bird's-eye view" photograph of Dawson.

will take prolonged and unflagging efforts upon the part of a whole brigade of lamps to dissipate the dark memories of this dismal winter in Dawson. Coal oil at $20 per gallon and threatening to rise to $35 is upsetting my usual equanimity. I only have two gallons, and four months of obscurity still lies ahead. Several of the neighbors have an expensive habit of coming to my cabin at night and bathing themselves for long periods of time in the radiance of my lamp. When they do depart without offering to settle their light bills, I promptly extinguish the flame and go to bed.

Although it is the middle of December and the thermometer fluctuates from 15 to 60 degrees below zero, the Yukon River is by no means solidly frozen over. A large area of open water lies just in front of my cabin and shows no signs of coating. The current is swift and the water evidently warm, as clouds of vapor are exhaled from it during cold days. The Klondike River nearby has a mid-winter peculiarity of overflowing the ice at its mouth, making the trail difficult between Klondike City and Dawson City. The other

Wells's photograph of "Main Street," Dawson.

day I attempted to cross the Klondike after one of these freshets and broke through the thin surface of new ice, sinking to my knees before I struck the second strata of solid ice.

Although I hurried to my cabin less than 500 feet away with all possible speed, my wet clothing was frozen solid before I could reach the door. Neither the Yukon nor the Klondike will be completely roofed with ice before February.

There are a number of bald-headed gentlemen in Dawson engaged in business, but not a single pretty typewriter girl to sit industriously by, reflecting the bewitching beauty of her countenance in one of those polished and hairless domes of knowledge. Yet there are several writing machines in the town, imported by the Healy company, and boys who are attempting to operate them

Wells's photograph of the Alaska Commercial Company store in Dawson.

earn from $8 to $10 per day. An excellent opening exists for a few experienced lady stenographers. At present they could command $15 to $20 per day. Please don't all come at once, ladies, but if you do come, make up your minds to avoid stampedes to the mines and stick strictly to business. Everybody, businessmen and their wives, clerks and the kitchen help, have been stampeding of late to all points of the compass, excited over false reports of gold discoveries.

A shocking tragedy occurred two days ago at Moose Hide Creek, a few miles below Dawson. J. J. Miles, aged 40, the bookkeeper of the Alaska Commercial Company, went on a stampede to the creek in question, hoping to secure a mining claim. He was accompanied by Chris Johnson. The two separated and began searching the

Wells's photograph of a typical dog-sled team (person unidentified).

gulch for vacant claims. An hour or two afterwards Johnson went in search of his friend and found the latter frozen stark and stiff and lying in the snow.

Word was speedily sent to Dawson and a sleigh came for the remains. The weather was not excessively cold and the doctors pronounced it a case of heart disease due to over-exertion.

Poor Mrs. Miles! A bride of less than a year, she married in Seattle and accompanied her husband on his trip to the Arctic Northwest in search of a fortune. She is now here grieving over her sudden and irreparable loss. Miles was a quiet, kindly man and popular among his associates. The funeral will take place today with the Reverend J. Hall Young, Presbyterian missionary, officiating.

Dyspeptic men, women and girls find that the Yukon atmosphere is a marvelous antidote for their distressing complaints, restoring the normal appetite, renewing the gastric juices and bringing back the bloom of youth to the jaded cheek. I believe this is the way the patent medicine people put it before affixing their price of $1 per bottle.

The Yukon atmosphere is not bottled up. It is plentiful and free to all. Lean men and attenuated women find it fat-producing to an alarming extent. Chubby cheeks and double chins have full sway and people all remark about it. Normally fat men living "down in the States" are liable to become abnormally fat by sojourning on the Yukon.

The truth of the matter is that the bracing atmosphere, fresh as the dew of an early spring morning, combined with healthful out-of-door exercise, camping, wood chopping and the like, is doing wonders for a multitude of persons who came here with their constitutions weakened and their nervous and vital energies at low ebb.

But mark you well! This is not the country for a finicky man! He who cannot or will not do for himself, who is afraid to use an ax and will not do his share of the cooking in camp or cabin, and looks for other people to wait on him, had better keep away. Effeminate men are the worst kind of baggage upon the frontier, and especially in the Arctic Northwest.

Christmas toys and barbershops are things that seem somewhat out of place upon the Yukon, yet one finds both in Dawson. A few years ago, when I first descended the great river of Alaska, silence and solitude reigned on both shores for 2000 miles. Black and brown bears were numerous on the mountainsides, and moose were plentiful in the somber forests. Now all is changed. There are fewer bears and more people. Stillness has given way to noise. Dawson's brass band plays "You Will Remember Me," while solitary fiddlers located along the Klondike are enlivening their cabin

Wells's photograph of typical aboveground storage as frequently used by Klondikers.

homes with strains from Sousa. The next thing I expect is to hear that one of E. O. McCormack's enterprising railroad agents has painted a "Big Four" sign upon the walls of the Grand Canyon. Then Lydia Pinkham will come in all her glory, and modern civilization will be here to stay.

As I stood, one morning earlier this month, near the counter in the Alaska Commercial Company's Store in Dawson, a crowd of adult Indians appeared and began inspecting the Christmas toys displayed upon the shelves. Chief Too-Much-Ice finally selected a woolly sheep on tin wheels, loudly grunting his satisfaction.

Another Wells photograph of Dawson, taken October 8, 1897. The large building is O'Brien's Trading Store, nearing completion.

Another chief picked out some tin men attached to painted iron wheelbarrows which they pushed along with active metallic legs. The Indians had plenty of money to pay for these things. I could not help wondering at the scene. Scarcely six years ago these same fierce Ayan Indians had met me near Pelly River attired in moose-skin garments. Now they were sadly degenerated, wearing store clothes and an Americanized aspect.

The squaws down at the Indian village, below Dawson, have each been earning from $20 to $40 per day this winter, making moccasins and gloves for the miners. Early in the season they caught on to the white man's game of charging big prices for every-thing, and it was not long before they went him one better. Moc-casins made out of moose hide, which formerly cost 6 bits, took a sudden jump to $5 a pair, and then to $7. The demand at $7 is currently very strong, and business is brisk. Gloves are scarce at $8, and poor makeshifts at that.[6]

[6]This concludes Wells's newspaper dispatches from Dawson. As mentioned in the letter to the Cincinnati *Post* preceding this article, Captain Ray sent urgent dis-patches to Captain John J. Healy, general manager of the North American Trading and Transportation Company, urging him to see that the letters were forwarded to the War Department in Washington, D.C., at once.

The difficulty of getting letters and papers safely out of Dawson to "the States" was well known to Captain Healy, as he had only a few weeks before paid a large sum of money to a man going out on other business over the winter trail for the safe delivery of business letters to Chicago. When Captain Ray's dispatches arrived, therefore, Captain Healy hardly knew what to do, as he stated to Wells.

Finally, Healy made Wells a proposition to carry out the dispatches. Healy told him that Wells's previous experience in winter traveling in Alaska made him feel that Wells could safely make the journey and deliver the letters. Even though Wells had no intention whatever of leaving Dawson before the following summer, he deferred to what he considered the importance of the dispatches, and agreed to undertake the journey for a fee to be determined later and paid by the government. Healy advanced him $1000 for traveling expenses, preparations were hurriedly made and Wells and company departed Dawson for Skagway on December 20, 1897, less than five days after he was approached by Captain Healy.

Since speed was of the utmost importance, and because Wells's journey from Dawson to Washington, D.C., was confidential in nature, Wells wrote no account of his journey for publication. The description which follows is a summary Wells pre-pared after he reached Cincinnati, from a diary he kept along the trail.

PART III

THE ESCAPE

It was on the twentieth day of December 1897 that I left Dawson, in the Northwest Territory, accompanied by three men and six dogs, to make the trip out over the Yukon winter trail to Skagway on the seacoast. My companions were Charlie Christiansen, a Swede; John Bigelow, an Australian; and Charlie Lake, a young man from Reno, Nevada. Our two sleds, each 8 feet long, were of the typical Yukon type and were loaded down with 1100 pounds of provisions, blankets and camp equipment, including a tent and sheet-iron stove.

Three Indian dogs, Fido, The Boy and Kodiak, were in the first team, drawing a load of some 600 pounds. The second team consisted of Billick, a full-blooded Eskimo, and two Newfoundlands, Klondike and Panto, the last-named a large and powerful animal who could pull 300 pounds steadily all day, and could himself start a sled, fully loaded, without assistance. The other dogs were good for 200 pounds apiece. Fido was a little dog of the short-haired Indian type with a vigorous progressive bark, and a tail that wagged sixty beats to the minute. The Boy was a surly, gloomy-faced canine, forever growling and snapping like a dyspeptic book-keeper, but with all was a hard worker. He was always spoiling for a fight and made friends with none of the dogs except Fido, whom he bit once in a while by way of variety. Kodiak was a big worthless fellow, lazy as a North American tramp, and always eager to get into camp. He invariably kept one eye back upon his driver and only buckled down to work when he saw a whip flourished in the air. Billick, the only Eskimo dog, with a heavy fur coat and a bushy wolf's tail, was a good worker and evinced an intelligent interest in proceedings. He prided himself upon his fighting abilities and soon began hostilities with The Boy, which continued at diverse times throughout the trip. The two were evenly matched. Klondike was a worker of the most tiresome description. He had a habit of doubling himself up in a bowknot when pulling, which had a most distressing effect upon beholders. Nobody liked Klondike because he always insisted upon pulling at the wrong time during the day and sleeping on top of the men of the party at night. It made little difference to him whether he camped upon their heads or their feet, and when kicked off would almost invariably return. Panto, the large Newfoundland, was a dignified dog, playfully inclined, however, and one of the very best workers in the team. He disliked whippings and seldom required any, being ready and very quick. When unhitched, Panto had a playful habit of hurling his 140 pounds of avoirdupois at anyone who was willing to play with him and not infrequently sent his man to the ground, or, rather, the snow.

John Bigelow had charge of the team headed by Billick, Christiansen handled the other, while Lake and I walked or ran behind as the case might be.

Our two sleds were of the usual low Yukon type, being constructed out of oak, with their beds only six inches above the runners, which were shod with inch-and-a-quarter iron. One of the sleds had a basket, so called, with steering handles elevated behind, but these were finally broken off and discarded.

Our equipment for the trip consisted of three fur robes, a wall tent 8 by 10, a sheet-iron stove having three lengths of pipe, four pairs of blankets, several sacks filled with extra clothing and moccasins, one rifle, a .45-90, and a miscellaneous collection of provisions, some seven hundredweight, consisting mainly of flour, bacon, beans, rice, sugar, tea, condensed milk, dried fruit, etc. The dogs were to be fed out of these supplies, their rations consisting of three pounds apiece of a mixture of pork and boiled flour, dished out every evening, before bedtime. These dogs usually had some dried salmon mixed into the feed to flavor it, as they have an especial fondness for fish.

The early morning was cloudy and warm when we pulled out of Dawson and headed up the snowy expanse of the Yukon River. It may be proper to say, however, that it was warm only by comparison with the usual severe winter temperatures; the thermometer hovered around the 20-degrees-below-zero mark. At first there was a well-beaten trail over smooth ice, but we soon reached a hummocky locality where the traveling was difficult. We made only ten miles before noon and then stopped for our first lunch in the snow. During the afternoon, snow began falling and then I witnessed the most wonderful optical illusion which I ever beheld in the country. The southern sun circling just above the hills burst through the clouds and sent a broad heavy band of yellow light like a gigantic bar from a mountain peak on the north side to another on the south, standing out in startling relief against a dazzling white background of falling snow. Had that yellow bar been real gold and not a spurious imitation, it would probably have been worth about a million dollars. But like the elusive jack-o'-lantern, we could not capture it. However, it may have been symbolical of the region and also a sign of good luck.

Our first camp was pitched in the snow about twenty miles from Dawson, and here we first had experience of the comforts and discomforts of sleeping out upon the winter trail. The little sheet-iron stove erected inside of the tent with its pipe projecting through a hole in the top was our greatest treasure, as it soon made a comfortable temperature in our living room. It was a good cooking stove, too, and on it we were able to prepare quite satisfactory meals. A little oven in the back served for baking biscuits of flour, water and baking powder, while the top was utilized for boiling and frying other things. Christiansen acted as cook for the table, having had previous professional experience, while Bigelow undertook the job of cooking for the dogs over a fire built outside in the snow. His was the colder and more cheerless job, keeping him busy late into the night. After supper, the fur robes and blankets were spread down in the end of the tent away from the stove with a few fir bows for springs and we soon dropped off into a restful sleep. With plenty of furs one can be most comfortable even under adverse winter conditions.

On Tuesday, December 21, we broke camp in the gray light of the early dawn and with a temperature no worse than that of the day previous continued our course up the Yukon River, still guided by a well-worn trail made by previous parties. Our mid-day lunch consisted of hot tea and fresh doughnuts which Christiansen had contrived to make the night before. A blinding snowstorm was raging all the while, powdering the doughnuts with imitation sugar even as we ate them. Snow fell all of the afternoon, making the trail difficult. We met quite a number of men coming and going in both directions, some being parties from Stewart River. We overtook and passed a self-sufficient member of the Canadian Parliament, whose traveling outfit consisted of two sleds and four dingy dogs. It was evident that he could make no speed, being three days out from Dawson already. This same gentleman had refused to take me with him on his trip out, being afraid of delay. I passed him with a formal bow which was returned in a frigid manner. There was a keen temptation to offer a tow rope, but I desisted. So far as I know, he is still upon the route coming out.

Late in the afternoon the pale purples of the Arctic light blending with the soft whiteness of the snow and the grayish tints of the spruces made an indescribably pretty picture. We camped that night in the woods where the snow was about one foot in depth. Our record for the day was eighteen miles. The dogs were tired from the hard day's work, and gladly took their opportunity to rest, sleeping out in the snow. Subsequently we allowed three of them camping accommodations inside of our comfortable tent, a concession which was evidently appreciated by them. It should be understood that every man in the party had to walk, the sleds being so heavily loaded as to preclude the possibility of carrying passengers.

On Wednesday, December 22, we broke camp shortly after daylight, at 9:20 A.M., and moved slowly upstream. Many people were encountered. The trail that afternoon was very heavy, owing to a fresh fall of light snow. A magnificent sunset began about 3 P.M. and developed into a long-drawn-out panorama of gorgeous coloring. The southeastern horizon turned livid with red fires, as though the earth had kindled into flames. Right in the center of this seething conflagration appeared a small island crowned with tall snow-white spruces, apparently defying the fires that raged about. A high mountain to the left, gray with snow and rocks blended together, was thrown bodily into the flaming cataclysm. Stately mountains garbed in white stood upon the northern horizon like gigantic specters gazing solemnly upon the scene. Away to the westward ran the dazzling white ribbon of the Yukon. The effect of the vision was grand and indescribable. That night we camped nine miles beyond Sixty Mile River, near a cabin where twenty-six other persons had stopped for the night. As we did not know our neighbors and were afraid lest some of our effects would be stolen, we pulled both of our sleds up the bank of the river and pitched our tent back on the edge of a dense forest where the snow was waist deep. Lake and I cut spruce boughs for beds, while Christiansen and Bigelow attended to tent and stove. That night we dried our footwear by suspending various articles from a string in the top of the tent. The weather continued warm and cloudy.

On Thursday, December 23, the skies were still overcast, with the temperature about 8 degrees below zero. The air was filled with a mist which continued all of the day. During the afternoon we met with our first serious misadventure. The guiding or "gee" pole of one sled had been broken going over a rough patch of ice and Bigelow and I had remained behind to fix it. A few minutes later we heard faint shouts ahead around a bend of the river where

Christiansen and Lake had disappeared with the remaining sled. When we reached the spot, a most distressing spectacle met our eyes. The ice had broken near the bank, dropping our sled into the water so that it was half submerged. Christiansen and Lake, assisted by the dogs, were pulling with might and main at the front end of the sled to prevent it from sinking further into the water, and were nearly exhausted. I saw at a glance that great damage had undoubtedly been done to our provisions and bedding. We made haste to assist in getting the sled out upon firm ice, the water upon the outside of the cargo freezing into ice almost instantly. Scarcely had the sled proceeded one hundred feet further, along the ice, before it gave way again and we barely escaped the loss of everything in the swift flood. A second rescue brought our cargo out in a very bad condition. What puzzled me was the fact that the ice seemed rotten although nearly half a foot in thickness at the points where the accidents occurred. Subsequently I discovered that there were many such treacherous places along the Yukon. The water of the river running swiftly beneath the ice was comparatively warm and was constantly eroding the undersurface of the ice, cutting it away during mild weather until nothing but a top shell of completely rotten character was left in places. A cold snap of 40 or 60 below would cause new ice to form, only to be cut away again when the temperature rose. After the accidents described, we quickly made camp in the first convenient woods, finding our blankets and fur robes wet and frozen, while the flour and sugar and other articles upon the sled were solid with ice. Much of our sugar was lost in the accidents. That night we slept in bedding stiffened by ice. My own robe was in perhaps the best condition, having only been saturated in spots. It was impossible to dry out the robes or bedding, as no bonfire could be built that was hot enough to drive away the moisture without holding the articles so close to the flames as to burn them. It was nearly a week before we reached the point where it was possible to dry the bedding.

On Friday, December 24, we broke camp at 8:50 A.M., with the thermometer indicating 20 degrees below zero. Two hours later we reached Henderson Creek and beheld rude signboards sticking up from out of the snow with inscriptions of various camps. One of these signs bore the legend "Dr. Smith, Physician." Alas, Dr. Smith was advertising! Perhaps he thought that the outside world would never hear of it. I have told on him, however, and the medical societies will doubtless turn the doctor down when he comes home for publishing his business in the Arctic snows.

We passed Henderson Creek, Stewart and White rivers, on this date, and camped late Christmas Eve in two feet of snow, opposite three large mountains. We had a late and very uncomfortable supper and finally sank off to sleep dreaming of the holidays.

Saturday was Christmas and the weather clerk sent the mercury to 34 below zero, but swept the sky clear of clouds for the first time in many days. During the mid-winter season, the sun circling low in the horizon is generally hidden beneath the mountains, but this day, as we traveled, there came a glorious burst of sunshine at high noon gleaming over the mountain peak and flashing a warm radiance into our faces. It was the first time for five weeks that we had seen the rubicund visage of old Sol. It seemed like a Christmas gift, that sunshine. Jack Frost, standing on the summit of one of the hills to the southward, could to all appearances have jabbed an icicle into the bottom of the sun, so close was the latter to the bottom of the hill. Our Christmas Day march was fourteen miles in length, and our camp was pitched in the spruce woods at 3 P.M.

Sunday, December 26, we sped up the stream some eighteen miles, for the Arctic traveler knows no rest. Provisions are scarce and delays are out of the question. The bushes were heavily covered with hoarfrost. That evening we camped beside the trail upon the river's ice. While supper was being prepared, Charlie Christiansen discovered a big timber wolf trotting down the trail toward our camp. He hurried into the tent to get my rifle to shoot the beast, which was scarcely a hundred yards away. The unpleasant discovery was made that the rifle was useless, owing to the plunge in the river several days before. The mechanism was full of ice. In

171

the meantime the wolf cut around the camp and disappeared in the darkness, while the dogs snarled and barked.

Monday, December 27, we made twenty-two miles, the weather being cloudy and comparatively warm. On this day about noon we reached a stranded meat raft where a considerable stock of frozen beef was cached, the owner having failed to reach Dawson with it before the ice closed in and stopped the river navigation. We dickered for some of the meat and finally secured about 70 pounds, for which we paid $56. The butcher was living in a tent nearby and had a number of Klondikers for neighbors. These had erected half a dozen cabins on an adjacent island, as they wanted to be near a base of supplies for the winter.

Tuesday, December 28, the skies were clear, with the thermometer 18 degrees below zero. One experience we had was typical of northern discomforts. Our biscuits baked that morning in the little stove became solidly frozen on the sled, and at noon when we came to a luncheon spot in the snow, we thawed these biscuits out, a layer at a time, over the fire, nibbling off the heated surface until our teeth crunched into the ice beneath, when another thawing of the dough became necessary. I secured a photograph of the two dog teams about noon, but the light was poor and the results unsatisfactory.

Wednesday, December 29, the temperature fell to 32 below zero, the skies being clear. It was a matter of common remark that on these clear days the thermometer invariably indicated extreme frigidity, whereas the appearance of clouds in the skies upon other days portended a rise in temperature. Late in the afternoon we met with a most exciting adventure. Bigelow was driving the lead sled not far from shore when suddenly the ice gave way and the sled broke through, but did not sink, being held partially upon firm ice by the tow rope and the dogs. As Bigelow was trying to extricate the sled, the ice beneath him suddenly opened up and he went into the icy current, thoroughly wetting one side of his body. By a dexterous twist he succeeded in pulling himself out and in a moment more was in safety. Not a moment was to be lost in securing a fire

This is the photograph Wells took of the two dog teams about noon on Tuesday, December 28, 1897—"the results unsatisfactory."

to prevent his being frozen. A bundle of sticks and a candle which had been carried for such an emergency were speedily kindled into a flame upon the snow by one of the party, while two of the others seized hold of Bigelow's fast-freezing footwear and pulled it off by main force. Dry socks and moccasins were handy and he jumped into these.

Owing to the packing of the sled, it was impossible to get at a complete suit of dry clothing without dangerous delay. Bigelow took a sudden resolve. Pelly River trading station was about seven miles ahead, and he said, "I'll have to make a run for it, boys. Before you can fish out that clothing I will freeze." He was already numbed with cold and, leaving his sled and everything else behind, he departed on a brisk run up the river. For a long time we could see his figure moving along shore and in and out of the ice hummocks. Finally he disappeared from view around a big bend of the river.

We extricated his sled, finding his cargo but little damaged, and started for the post. The road became very rough and, to make matters worse, night came down upon us while we were yet miles away. Then the two teams got separated, Lake having charge of the one which Bigelow had deserted. The moon came up and aided us or we never could have reached the post that night. When we finally straggled in about five o'clock, Lake was there with his sled. We also found Bigelow in safety. The latter had barely escaped with his life. His experiences on that wild run of seven long miles were thrilling.

"I felt my clothing even to my shirts freezing stiff upon me," he said, "and I thought at one time that I would stop and build a fire. I tried it and flashed several matches in vain. I rapidly grew numb, and knowing that it was a desperate case, I again started on a race for the post not daring to make any more stops. Gradually my right arm grew insensible to the cold and I knew that it was next to freezing. You can imagine how glad I was when I finally turned one bend in the river, just at nightfall, and saw the smoke of cabins ahead. When I reached the place, the post trader, Pitkey, at once took me in and I have been thawing here ever since."

There were several vacant cabins at the post, one of which was assigned to us for our use overnight. As both Indians and whites had camped in it for many months, I suspected that the place swarmed with vermin and was loath to sleep there, but there was no help for it. Our fur robes and bedding were filled with ice, Bigelow's clothing had to be dried, and so did these other things. We therefore stretched lines through the cabin and began a slow drying-out process, using a small iron stove which we found in the cabin to raise the temperature.

The next morning, December 30, the thermometer indicated 40 below zero. It was the last day on which I was able to secure any such observations. An inquisitive Indian trying to inspect my thermometer knocked it down from its perch on the outside of the cabin and smashed it. Another catastrophe occurred later on in the day. Some unknown person, presumably an Indian of the village, inflicted a bad wound upon one of our dogs. The animal was discovered bleeding profusely from a cut in the back within a stone's throw of the cabin. He lost such quantities of blood that we believed his death to be only a matter of a few hours. At once there was trouble in camp. The dog had not only cost me $250 but was almost indispensable to our progress. I called on trader Pitkey in company with Charlie Christiansen, who had his Swedish blood up to the fighting point, and we demanded an immediate investigation of the outrage. There were only six buck Indians at the place and these we proceeded to put on the carpet without delay. Christiansen boldly threatened to hang the Indian who had perpetrated the deed, if he could catch him. They all denied knowledge of the affair and we were finally compelled to give up the investigation, although there was no doubt but that one of them was the guilty party. The act disturbed us not a little, as it indicated an unfriendly disposition, and we took care to gather up all of our dogs and put them in places of safety for the night.

While at the post we repaired one of our badly broken sleds and discarded the other one, which was worthless, buying a good new one from the trader to take its place. Although we had traveled but 170 miles since leaving Dawson ten days before, the roughness of the ice had played smash with our equipment.

On Friday, December 31, the last day of the year, a remarkable phenomenon occurred. The temperature overnight had been rapidly rising and by morning was almost spring-like in its mildness. Trader Pitkey had a thermometer of his own and it indicated 20 degrees above zero, as against 40 below on the previous evening—a change of 60 degrees inside of twelve hours. Violent gusts of wind blew in our faces, coming from upriver. We did not care to stop longer, being obliged to husband our provisions, and we made preparations to start. The injured dog unexpectedly turned up alive, although very weak. One mishap at this post I have failed to note. We had depended upon finding 60 pounds of dried salmon there, which Bigelow had left with the trader when descending the river the previous fall. Nigger Jim and party, coming out from Dawson a few days ahead of us, had discovered the presence of this salmon and had presented a fraudulent order for it, which the trader had accepted. After a stormy argument with Bigelow, the trader determined to help us out by turning over a 60-pound can of dog tallow, for which he charged us $30. The arrangement was manifestly an unfair one to us, but we were obliged to make the best of it as there was no law in the place and we did not care to proceed to the extremity of robbing the trader of his tallow by force of arms, although we would probably have been justified in so doing. We hitched up our dogs and took our departure in the early morning, with Christiansen hurling a few words of angry farewell at the buck Indians clustered upon the bank of the river. The trail was very rough and bad and the wind blew furiously, drifting the snow and making our progress slow and difficult. The dog that had been injured was sick but we were obliged to work him in the traces, although he pulled but little. As we progressed, the winter trail became so buried under the swirling snow that we lost it altogether at times. Just above the trading post, Pelly River entered from the east and we found a horrible jam of ice for some miles.

The furious blasts of the wind produced a peculiar effect upon the landscape. The snow-laden spruces of the forest, which presented a soft gray effect to the eye, blending their color harmoniously with the white expanse of the river and the red streakings of the sky, were now disrobed and stood out in a bold green nakedness that destroyed all of the picturesque effect. In fact, one could not admire the millinery bonnet of green, red and white which Nature now saw fit to adopt.

During the afternoon I hurt my right foot by stumbling against an ice hummock and the accident made it necessary for us to go into camp at 2 P.M.

New Year's Day of 1898 was ushered in by a beautiful red sunrise, the most magnificent that I had ever witnessed. It looked as though the world were burning up and reflecting its fires into the heavens above. My foot was still lame but we made a start at ten o'clock, finding to our discouragement that the wind of the day previous had almost completely demolished the trail. To make matters much worse, the snow was crusty, so that it impeded the progress of the sleds and greatly worried the dogs. A vast sea of ice hummocks stretched away upriver. We wound in and out among them, finding the passage very rough, and there were frequent catastrophies such as the upsetting of sleds. We made only four miles during the morning and ate our New Year's dinner of frozen biscuits, butter and tea while standing in the snow. In the afternoon we got blocked by going up a side channel of the river where the ice had sunk beneath the water and were compelled to beat a retreat and tediously cut away around an island into the main channel of the river. Late in the day we met J. B. Burnham, business manager of the sporting periodical *Field and Stream*. He and his partner were pulling their own sleds out to Juneau. Burnham photographed us. The weather was cloudy and very warm. We only made two miles during the afternoon, cutting our way through the ice hummocks with axes. Soon after we had gone into camp, the wind rose to a gale and blew fiercely all through the night.

January 2, the sky was clear and the weather warm. We broke camp at 9 A.M. and found the trail difficult. On this day we only made twelve miles. On January 3, we made an unusually early start, getting underway at eight o'clock, when there was just barely light enough to find the trail. The snow underfoot was like pulverized sugar and would not pack, making travel slow and difficult. In some places the trail improved, however, over previous days. We observed wolf tracks in the snow in front of us. The wind continued warm, blowing in from the coast, which was about 180 miles away in an air line. The temperature was barely below the freezing point, and the waters of the river had cut completely through the ice at many points. The day was notable from the fact that we saw the sun for the first time since Christmas. Our record for the day was about fifteen miles. The dogs barked all night, perhaps scenting wolves.

On January 4, we again started at eight o'clock, finding very rough ice as we approached Five Finger Rapids. The weather was much colder, the sky again being clear. It might be well to describe how we made our camp that night just beyond the rocks of the Five Fingers. It was a typical camp. At 3:30 P.M. we turned the dogs out of the trail and headed them up into the woods. Darkness was slowly gathering over the forest. We drove one team with a sled containing the bedding up the bank of the river to the spot where we had decided to pitch our tent. Lake at once seized an ax and began to cut firewood. I took another ax, felled a spruce tree and began to trim off branches for the beds. Christiansen and Bigelow, in the meantime, put up the tent, which was a difficult job, owing to the fact it was partly frozen. Then the boughs which I had cut were thrown into the interior for a floor and the bedding taken from the sled dumped upon it. The little sheet-iron stove, placed upon two cross logs in the tent with three joints of pipe projecting through the roof, was filled with dry spruce and a fire kindled, which soon produced a comforting warmth. Our beds were spread out and then supper was cooked by Christiansen. In the meantime, Bigelow had built another fire outside of the tent and was boiling the dog food, consisting of flour and bacon in several gallons of water. The six dogs sat in a solemn circle around this kettle, watching the proceedings and fully understanding that their supper was in preparation. Occasionally one would pull himself a little closer to the kettle in order to get a more satisfactory sniff at the contents. Then the others would bark angrily as a warning that he must retreat.

One noteworthy incident of the afternoon was the discovery of two wolves who were watching us as we attempted to make a difficult river crossing where the ice was weak. These big fellows sat upon the side of a hill within easy rifle range and did not seem alarmed at our presence. As fortune would have it, the rifle was packed in the bottom of one of the sleds and we were compelled to put up with their impudence without a bombardment.

On January 5, clear and mild weather prevailed. During the

morning we reached a cluster of cabins and discovered the first evidences of disaster to preceding travelers upon the river. In one of the cabins lay William Byrne, of Chicago, aged 17, minus both of his feet. He had frozen them and a doctor named Bicket, of Seattle, had performed an amputation to save his life. The story of Byrne's adventures was a horrible one. In company with his uncle, he had been traveling with a sled up the river, and one day had broken through the ice and wet his feet. Instead of at once changing his footwear, he pushed ahead with his uncle and his feet became partly frozen. The two men had a tent but no stove, and Byrne did not take off his frozen moccasins at night but traveled along in them day after day, his feet gradually solidifying. Finally the big toe of one foot came through the moccasin and the flesh was worn off to the bone. A party of men coming by observed the terrible condition of the lad and brought him to the camp where we found him. There were threats of lynching the uncle for his inhumanity, and he speedily left for the seacoast. Several of the Klondikers undertook to nurse the unfortunate boy until spring, when he could be rafted down to Dawson.

On January 6, our expedition reached and passed McCormack's Post, making a twenty-mile journey over trail that was both good and rough at times. The temperature was apparently about 10 below zero. Fine and clear weather now prevailed.

On January 7, at two o'clock in the afternoon, we reached the Canadian government post at Little Salmon River, in charge of Captain Cortland Stearns. The policemen received us kindly and asked for our names to be entered upon their register. The book showed that 301 persons had already passed on the winter trail going out toward the seacoast and it was said that probably 50 others had passed by who had not registered. There were several reasons for keeping this register. It was a record showing who had passed so that in case of future accidents they could be traced up. Furthermore, it revealed the fact that assistance in the way of provisions had been given to various travelers at this post. It may be stated right here that the Canadian Northwest Mounted Police did much

179

by the free distribution of provisions to avert starvation on the Yukon trail during the winter. Had it not been for them scores of persons might have perished. The plan adopted was to give free provisions to all who applied at the Yukon posts in need of assistance. These same provisions were obtained by the police in various ways, some of the supplies having been brought in at great expense by mule trains, while others had been purchased from miners at the rate of $1 and even $2 per pound. The police were just establishing their stations and two were contemplated on Little Salmon, while others were to be placed at the mouths of various tributaries of the Yukon River.

That night we camped in a dugout at the mouth of Little Salmon, finding a community of sixteen men and one woman, housed in cabins. One man was selling his outfit in preparation for departure to the seacoast, and from him I obtained five candles for the trifling sum of $5. Candles were a necessity while traveling in making and breaking camp. Prospect holes had been sunk at various points near this camp and developed a few colors of gold, but no big strikes were reported.

On January 8, early in the morning I had a unique and exciting experience in the dugout. My heavy chinchilla coat had been hanging behind the little stove, and at breakfast time I took it down and sat upon it, for a seat. A few moments later Lake remarked, "Something is burning." But I ate on. After breakfast was over, I picked up my coat and found it a mass of fire at the tails. One pocket had burned out entirely; the other side pocket, which contained my diary and memorandum books, had escaped. When I finally extinguished the conflagration, the garment was a sight to behold, but I was compelled to don it. On this day we made twenty miles.

January 9 was chiefly notable for the fact that at 3:30 P.M. we reached Big Salmon River and found there Major Walsh, who was the Canadian official sent out to take supreme command of the Northwest Territory. At his request, I spent the evening with him in his tent. He said, "I have issued an order that no persons except couriers shall be allowed to pass Tagish Lake unless they have with them three pounds of food per day for one year to the man. This is the only plan that I know of to avert starvation. I have asked the Canadian government to request the U.S. in cooperating with Canada to exclude people without food. I have been assisting Americans and Canadians impartially, as well as all others who have applied.''

Major Walsh was slightly gray, of medium height and spare build. He has a pleasant address. As I was departing he asked my needs and gave me four candles, three pounds of sugar and a quarter pound of baking powder, for which he would receive no money. He intended, he said, to remain at Big Salmon for a while, rather than go down to Dawson, in order to better control the situation at both ends.

On January 10, we made an early start from Big Salmon, traveling toward the Hootalinqua and making some eighteen miles.

January 11. This morning I found ice in my watch under the crystal; how it got there, I cannot imagine. One of the hands had been broken off, and in attempting to open the case to get out the ice, I broke off the other hand. Strange to say, the works of the watch were not affected and it continued to do good duty as a timepiece, although I had difficulty in determining the hour of the day with the two little stubs of the hands. It was on this day we reached the Hootalinqua.

January 12 was the first of three troublesome days. We started up that portion of the Yukon River known as Thirty Mile, which was very swift and was not frozen over, although shore ice could be found in many places along the banks. It was a terrific struggle. We were obliged to abandon the river in many places and work our way up and down through the hills. The dogs were exhausted and so were the men. Whenever a bit of shore ice offered along which we could travel, we made slightly better progress, but the day closed with only about nine miles accomplished.

January 13 found us still struggling along Thirty Mile, with the trail worse than ever before. Part of the time we scrambled over rough hillsides and again along sloping shore ice, where we held the sleds up by hand and by using ropes to prevent them from sliding into the river. On this day we scarcely made five miles.

On January 15 we struck the worst portion of the entire trail. It lay all of the way along the edge of a precipitous bluff with a scanty fringe of sloping shore ice, which was rotten and breaking away in a good many places. On several occasions it gave way beneath our feet. We had to use the greatest care to prevent the sleds from toppling over into the water. At 11 A.M. we reached Lake Laberge, having finally completed this toilsome portion of our journey, and once more found the ice firm and traveling good. Here we found a station of the Canadian Mounted Police and were given fifteen pounds of bacon for our dogs. At 12:45 P.M., we started across Laberge, which is about thirty miles in length by six to twelve miles broad, intending to make a run of sixteen miles to a certain point. Christiansen and Bigelow drove the two teams while Lake and I walked behind. The trail was good and so the two of us allowed the sleds to pull ahead to a considerable distance while we followed leisurely behind. This proved to be bad policy. Gradually the night descended while we were still far out upon the lake and distant many miles from our objective point. Still, Lake and I did not trouble ourselves as we noticed the sleds disappearing far ahead in the gloom. The trail was a plain one and we felt competent to follow it even on the darkest night. But now an unexpected situation arose. A wind sprung up and the fine snow began to drift into the trail, blown off the surface of the lake. The temperature steadily fell. As soon as I noticed the drifting of the snow, I became alarmed, and called Lake's attention to it. He started to run but I called him back, telling him to keep a cool head. There was danger that we would become separated, and that might prove fatal under these circumstances. It would never do to get lost upon the big lake with the temperature far below zero and the wind fast rising to a gale. Painfully and slowly we followed the now fast-disappearing track, straining our eyes in the gloom to get its general direction. By and by the stars began to twinkle in the heavens and the darkness of night came down upon the white surface of

182

Laberge. We could no longer see the trail. It had disappeared in the drifting snow and darkness. "Charles," said I, "we must strike for shore at once. Both of us are getting chilled. We cannot find the dogs tonight and must stand it until morning over a fire." Fortunately we had matches in our pockets and, striking a beeline at right angles to our former course, guided by the dim outlines of the mountains, which we could still see cutting the skies ahead, we finally reached the edge of the lake and found ourselves near a rocky bluff around which the winds were swirling with an ever increasing energy. We stumbled along in the darkness, hunting the lee side of the rocks so as to get out of the wind, and then began fumbling in the snow for driftwood, which we soon found to be quite plentiful, the summer storms having cast large quantities of timber upon the point. Most of it was frozen into the ice, however, and was totally inaccessible, except the projecting branches. We had no ax, but managed to break off a number of dry twigs and with numbed fingers I struck a match, which produced a tiny blaze that was soon kindled into a fire by careful manipulation. Anxious, we fed it with little sticks at first, and then piled on larger limbs as the flames grew stronger. How we hugged that bit of warmth! It was the only thing that stood between us and freezing. We had no blankets and there was no such thing as camping, especially as the snow was fully two feet deep.

Our next step was to gather sufficient firewood for the night before we became too weary, and this was accomplished but not without difficulty. Our fire had been built beneath the spreading branches of a dead spruce tree which later in the night served as a partial shelter, when the snow began to fall. It was about six o'clock in the evening when we built our fire and twelve long mortal hours of darkness lay ahead. How slowly the time passed. Every few minutes I looked at the watch to see how the night progressed. We dared not go to sleep even while lying close up to the cheerful blaze. We arranged some boughs upon the snow, however, and stretching out upon them with our faces to the fire and our backs freezing cold, we proceeded to endure as best we could. Early in the evening we looked for signal fires down the lake kindled by our missing companions but were puzzled to see none. A half dozen dry spruces nearby were kindled by torches and sent immense columns of flames and sparks in the sky as beacons, but there was no answering light. So we had to grin and bear it as best we might. Slowly the hours of the night dragged on. A number of times my chinchilla coat caught fire from too close proximity to the blaze, but I extinguished the blaze with a little snow. As morning gradually dawned, we looked anxiously out toward the lake, preparing to start as soon as we could see our way. Both of us were faint and hungry, having had no supper the night before. About 7 A.M. the light was sufficiently strong for us to get underway and we started boldly out across the lake, not attempting to find any trail but heading in the direction which we supposed our companions had gone. Miles after miles we traversed in this fashion and the heavens grew brighter. The full day appeared and yet there were no signs of Bigelow and Christiansen and the missing teams. The wind rose. Lake began to complain of the cold and we decided to strike in toward the timber skirting the shore, where we could build a fire if we became benumbed. About ten o'clock, amidst the drifting of the snows occasioned by the wind, we saw appearing ahead of us a procession of large objects of singular appearance. ''Those are too big for our dog teams,'' exclaimed Lake. We moved toward them and discovered horses drawing large sleds loaded with provisions. It was an equipment of the Canadian Mounted Police. I promptly went up to one of the officers, told him we were half famished and begged a meal. He pointed to a tent nearby on the shore where the police had encamped overnight. We proceeded to it and secured much-needed refreshment. We were informed that our dogs and sleds had passed not fifteen minutes before going toward the foot of the lake. We followed after them, feeling considerably better, and after a long and tiresome tramp, at 2:30 P.M. found Christiansen and Bigelow with the dogs at a hut at the foot of the lake awaiting our arrival. They had become uneasy and were planning a search of the lake. I was not in good humor over their apparent desertion, but we finally smoothed matters out upon their statement that they had not known just what course to take.

January 17's run was a good one. We proceeded twenty-three miles up the Yukon over that stretch of it known as Sixty Mile, reaching the Whitehorse. We found the rapids open at one point but ice covered the waters for most of the distance. I discovered three tramways in course of construction for the summer traffic of 1898. These roadways, built along the sides of the mountains on either bank of the river, were three and one-half miles in length, beginning above the Grand Canyon of the Yukon and extending below the rapids. Wooden rails were to be used, placed on sleepers, like an ordinary railroad track. The tramcars, which were not yet constructed, were intended to convey loaded skiffs from the terminal above to the canyon below the bad water.

In the morning of January 18 we passed the canyon. I found it partially closed with ice along its walls but open more or less in the center. On this day we only made fourteen miles, owing to my lameness, caused by a blow received on the ice. We made camp in the woods. The river was noticeably narrowing.

On January 19, we reached Lake Marsh and had dinner at 2 P.M. at a little log hotel at $1.50 per head. The meal was a good one and gave evidence that we were approaching civilization. Here we met the vanguard of the incoming host of Klondikers sleighing their supplies over the ice. Some of them had erected masts and sails and were taking advantage of a favoring wind to glide almost without effort to the foot of the lake. After dinner we pushed on some six miles up Lake Marsh, finally camping in a desolate snowbank upon the shore. The winds howled this night most persistently, threatening to tear down our tent.

The following day, January 20, we finished Lake Marsh, tramping through considerable snow, and proceeded over on Tagish Lake, where we found the Canadian customs headquarters, in charge of Collector John Goodson. He furnished me with some necessary provisions. Information was vouchsafed that no miners would be allowed to enter the country henceforth who did not have at least 1000 pounds of provisions apiece, not counting tea, coffee and candles.

I have neglected to state one little incident which occurred on Lake Marsh shortly before reaching Goodson's station. We encountered a convoy of Stick Indians, with sleds and dogs and two women, proceeding toward the foot of the lake. The bucks had some hardtack in a box and after a little dickering I secured six of the crackers for $1.

January 21 saw us across Tagish Lake and encamped at Caribou Crossing. On this day we also passed many Klondikers pulling their sleds into the country.

On January 22 we had the toughest experience of our entire trip: crossing Lake Bennett, a distance of twenty-eight miles. For most of the distance the snow was crusted and in many places water-soaked, owing to cracks in the ice, which had allowed the moisture to well up from below. This wet snow freezing to our moccasins soon made them like cakes of ice. The further we progressed, the worse the traveling became and it was long after dark when we wearily pulled into McCloud's Town at the head of the lake. This was the point where we were to leave the Yukon and strike across the mountains forty miles to the seacoast. McCloud had a large cabin for a bunk room with a good board floor. I shall never forget the luxury of that first night under a roof in the genial warmth thrown out by a large fire. For over a month, we had been camping in the snow under the most adverse conditions. Having plenty of room, we spread our bunks upon the floor and lolled in luxury. I could not sleep that night. It was too comfortable and the sensation of being indoors was too novel. We secured our breakfast next morning from McCloud at the comparatively cheap price of $1 per head. It was stated that there were a large number of people living in cabins nearby. The Canadian Mounted Police also had a station there.

On January 23 we struck out through the mountains for Skagway, making eight miles and stopping for the night at Harry Pittock's cabin near the trail. During this eight-mile tramp we found an excellent trail beaten down through the snow to a depth of about four feet. Frequently we encountered packhorses bearing provisions and several sleds drawn by horses. There were numerous cabins along the route where Klondikers of the preceding fall had made their winter camps. Pittock stated to me that he was from Warren, Ohio. He had left six children and a wife behind in the Buckeye State. Two of his boys were at college and two of the girls were of an age when, as Pittock stated, they needed money for finery. The father of this family was clearing from $15 to $20 a day bunking and feeding travelers. He had six bunks, which he rented at 50 cents a night apiece, and charged $1 for meals. Many traders stopped with him. He stated that there were about fifty packers on the trail operating about fifteen packtrains. The rates for freight from the seacoast to Lake Bennett had dropped to 40 cents, having been as high as 75 cents a pound a few weeks previously.

January 24 was a glorious day. On it we made the greatest run of the trip, traveling through fog, sleet and snow a distance of thirty-two miles and tumbling or rolling into Skagway about eight o'clock at night. At least, two of us got there, Christiansen and I. Lake and Bigelow gave out and stopped eight miles up the canyon, to resume their trip the next morning. Christiansen and I, although desperately tired, were determined to make salt water. We started with the dogs and sled in a helter-skelter race down the steep inclines. Most of the way the trail followed the course of a mountain stream—the Skagway—sometimes upon the ice, again along the bank and occasionally scaling the mountainside. The night came down upon us but our journey was unchecked. Most of the time I rode upon the top of the cargo of the sled. At one point where there was a steep descent Christiansen took hold of the gee pole of the sled in front and braced his feet in the snow, while I hung on to a hold-back rope astern, sitting in the snow in order to act as a more efficient brake. The dogs were kept ahead. Down the declivity we went at terrific speed, the snow flying up in my face in clouds as I hung desperately on to the rope in my hands. Almost by a miracle, we landed safely at the bottom without mishap more serious than running over two dogs which could not keep out of the way. They were not injured except in their feelings. Soon it became so dark that we could not see the trail ahead and, to make matters more interesting, the river ice became treacherous, large open places being encountered where the rapid water surged beneath with a dull sullen roar. We were obliged to trust to the instincts of the dogs to keep the trail and to keep us out of the holes and right well did they perform their task. Finally we saw ahead the glimmer of the first lights upon the outskirts of Skagway and were soon driving into town, where we stopped in front of a hotel and were speedily surrounded by a crowd. I soon ascertained that the steamer *Rosalie,* in port, would leave early in the morning for Seattle and determined to go to "the States" on her. Purchasing necessary new clothing, securing a bath and needed refreshment took until after eleven o'clock that night. I slept but little. The bed was too comfortable.

Christiansen decided to remain for a while at Skagway, but in the early morning he assisted me down to the wharf with my baggage, Billick pulling the sled unassisted.

The voyage south began at 8 A.M. on January 25, and we reached Seattle late in the evening of January 31.

PART IV
THE AFTERMATH

Seattle, Washington, February 1, 1898 (Seattle Post-Intelligencer*)*

On the steamer *Rosalie,* which arrived from Alaska last night at ten o'clock, came E. H. Wells, a newspaperman who left Dawson December 20 and made the trip to tidewater in thirty-five days with three companions. Mr. Wells is the bearer of important dispatches to the War Department regarding Captain Ray and the situation at Fort Yukon. His mission is a secret one, and he will not divulge the nature of it.

Mr. Wells's three companions stopped at Juneau, and he was the sole Klondiker on the *Rosalie.* He states that Major Walsh has issued an order forbidding any Klondikers from entering Canadian territory on the Yukon from the coast without being supplied with at least 1000 pounds of food, exclusive of tea and coffee. This order was made effective January 15.

Like many well-posted men that have emerged from the Yukon, Mr. Wells believes that there is not enough food in Dawson to feed the people there. He declares that the number that came out over the trails is less than was supposed; that only 401 persons had passed Major Walsh on January 15 on their way out to the coast, whereas it was currently believed in Dawson that at least 1000 people had left the camp by that route.

191

The *Rosalie* brought eleven passengers and no other important northern advice. She left Skagway last Tuesday.

Mr. Wells, who was a member of the Arkell expedition, headed by E. J. Glave in 1890, was found at the Butler last night. He readily gave an account of the situation in Dawson when he left there. "I am the last man out of the Klondike," he said. "The last parties ahead of me were those of which W. M. Rank, Nigger Jim Doherty, Fred Stevens, Medlock and Bettles were members. The most important information I can give you is that on January 15, Major Walsh, the Canadian Gold Commissioner at Big Salmon, issued an order which he told me he desired spread far and wide to the effect that he would not allow men to enter the Yukon country on Canadian soil unless they were supplied with at least 1000 pounds of food, exclusive of tea and coffee. He had already turned back a number of people, and I have reason to believe that many others now crossing the divide will be stopped by him.

"There are no new developments as to the food situation at Dawson. So different are the views and opinions held as to that matter that I do not wish to be quoted at any length. I do not believe, however, that there is enough food to keep the people of the camp in health this winter. It is my belief that the government relief expedition should proceed with all possible dispatch.

"Reports of rich strikes on Hunker, Dominion and Sulphur creeks were brought to Dawson a few days before I left. From reliable parties I have gathered that the prospects on these streams are fully as good as those found on El Dorado and Bonanza at a similar stage of development.

"I crossed the Skagway trail, which I found in excellent shape owing to the good sledding. There were at least 500 people crossing the summit when I came over. Coming out from Pelly River, a severe blizzard had obliterated the trail made by those in advance of us, and for over 300 miles we had to break a road for ourselves. This made traveling slow and difficult.

"There are not to exceed twenty-five or thirty people coming out after us. There will be less and less use of the trail until the weather conditions change."

Mr. Wells was asked concerning the claim made by Arkell to an interest in the Klondike gold fields by right of discovery by the Arkell party. He said that the facts had been misrepresented by writers whose matter had been published after his departure for the gold fields last summer.

"I was somewhat surprised upon reaching the coast," he said, "to find that articles had been published during my absence in the interior of Alaska, in which the claim was made that Arkell's Alaska expedition in 1890–91 had discovered the Klondike, and that E. J. Glave, Schanz and myself had staked off the most valuable claims on the river. Mr. Arkell was certainly laboring under a misapprehension if he made such statements. Glave never saw the Yukon River, either upon the occasion of his first or his second visit to Alaska.

"The Arkell expedition left New York in 1890, with the following personnel: A. B. Schanz, E. J. Glave and myself. We proceeded to San Francisco, where Jack Dalton, the noted frontiersman, was added to the party; also Frank Price, a sailor who had had some experience in Arctic travel. The United States coast survey steamer *Patterson* conveyed us to Pyramid Harbor, Alaska, where Chilkat Indian Schwatka was engaged as an additional retainer. Other Indians to the number of twenty-six were hired, and the party started across the Chilkoot Pass, following a new route, which had never been traversed by white men. On the far side of the mountains a large lake was discovered, and subsequently named Arkell. The smaller lake was named Maude. While upon Lake Arkell it was decided to divide the party. By agreement between Mr. Glave and myself, he took Dalton, crossed over the divide to the Alsek River and descended to Dry Bay, on the Pacific Coast, having made a circuit of scarcely 200 miles from where he left salt water until he returned.

"Glave mapped the Alsek, discovered a few colors of gold in the

193

sands and returned to New York, where he urged Mr. Arkell to out-fit him again for a prospecting trip upon the Alsek. Mr. Arkell, so Glave wrote me, declined to enter upon the scheme. It had no rela-tion, however, to the Klondike country. In the meantime, Schanz, Price, Schwatka and myself built a raft, crossed Lake Arkell, descended the Takhena River to the Yukon, then drifted down the last-named stream to Forty Mile Creek. On this trip Schanz was taken seriously ill, and when we passed the mouth of the Klondike we made no stop at all, but hurried on toward our destination, which was the camp of the United States coast survey party, under Turner and McGrath, just below Forty Mile. Here we left Mr. Schanz in the care of the physician attached to the party. Three weeks later, when he had recovered sufficiently to travel, he descended the Yukon River, never returning upstream to the Klon-dike, but going out at the mouth of the Yukon to St. Michael. Later he made a trip down the coast in a bidarka to Nushagak, and then by dog team made his way in company with trader John Clark to the southern coast of Alaska. He discovered on the way a large lake, which he named Lake Clark.

"Meanwhile, after leaving Schanz at Forty Mile, Price, Schwatka and I made an overland journey to the headwaters of the stream and proceeded thence to the mountainous district lying northwest of Mount Wrangell, where the Kuskokwim heads. Our provisions were exhausted, and we were obliged to eat the one dog that had been taken along with the party, and with roots, rose pods, etc., managed to exist for six weeks while making our way westward toward the Tanana. We drifted down the Tanana to the Yukon, and thence to St. Michael. The *Bear* was to call for us, but we reached there eight days after the *Bear* had touched and left. Finding that it would be necessary to remain ten months at St. Michael while awaiting the arrival of another ship, I preferred the alternative of traveling down the coast by bidarka and did so, reaching Nushagak in November 1890.

"At Nushagak dogs were secured and we proceeded to Katmai, where we overtook Schanz. The party then crossed the Shelikof

Strait to Kodiak Island, and from there sailed for Sitka and the States.

"Not a single member of the party knew anything about the Klondike, nor did we make any gold discoveries. Our work was confined altogether to the mapping of rivers and lakes and mountain chains in the interior of Alaska. We did not have three Indians die on our hands, as alleged by one writer, and consequently Mr. Arkell did not have to pay $1000 each to their relatives. After our return, Glave and Dalton made another trip to Alaska, but did not enter the Yukon country, confining their researches to the Alsek River. They failed to find gold in any quantity. Mr. Arkell had no connection with this second enterprise. I leave you to judge from this statement as to whether the Arkell party can claim any right of discovery in the Klondike. I wish to have the truth stated in this matter."

Following is a list of the *Rosalie*'s passengers: H. Chandler and wife, J. H. Loomis, E. H. Wells, H. H. Buell, C. Peterson, I. McCormack, L. P. Lundberg, A. J. Chambers, John Johnson and S. Harris.

The steamer *Rosalie,* which arrived from Skagway and Dyea last night, will leave for the north again tonight on time.

Portland, Oregon, February 1, 1898

I started for Vancouver Barracks Monday under the following telegraphic instructions from Washington, D.C.:

> E. Hazard Wells, Seattle: The Acting Secretary of War directs that you take the dispatches you have from Captain Ray for the War Department to General Merriam, commanding the department at Vancouver Barracks, and deliver to him. It is very important that he get them as soon as possible. Acknowledge receipt.
>
> Samuel Breck
> Adjutant General

I delivered the dispatches today to General Merriam, and also specific verbal information on the scarcity of food in the Yukon country. The government relief expedition is an excellent project, and can be carried through successfully.

Major J. M. Walsh, commanding officer of the Canadian government on the Yukon River, met me at Big Salmon River. He said he hoped the United States would forward relief provisions, and he would do all in his power to help.

My mission relates to the scarcity of provisions in Alaska, where there are large numbers of Americans wintering. Hundreds of these are going to be forced to flee to Dawson, hoping for food. Few more persons cannot leave Dawson for the seacoast, as the supply of dogs has given out even at $300 per dog.

Unless the United States government takes steps to provision Alaska for next summer and establishes military rule everywhere, distressing results will ensue.

Thousands of Americans are preparing to invade the Tanana country of central Alaska, where good prospects of gold are reported and no royalties are exacted, as in Canada.

There is no food on the Tanana. The river is 800 miles long and has never been ascended by steamboat. Only two exploring parties, one headed by Lieutenant Allen, of the United States Army, and the other by myself in 1890, have ever descended the river. Allen and I are the only two men who know whether the Tanana is navigable.

The Yukon traders at Dawson have recently besieged me for information concerning this Tanana River and the possibility of getting provisions up it to supply the overland rush of prospectors from Dawson next spring.

The Tanana heads only 200 miles from Dawson and cuts the heart of the gold-bearing belt. I could navigate it.

Chicago, February 8, 1898 (Chicago Times*)*

E. H. Wells, the special carrier of dispatches for the United States government, who was sent from the Alaska gold fields by Captain Ray, U.S.A., in charge of the troops there, with dispatches for the Secretary of War, arrived in Chicago yesterday on his way to Washington. The dispatches, which were intercepted at Vancouver Barracks, Washington, by General Merriam, acting under orders from Washington, D.C., were given publicity in condensed form.

Wells brought letters from the officials of the North American Transportation and Trading Company at Dawson City to the head office in this city. The letters support the urgent need outlined in Captain Ray's dispatches of a strong force of United States soldiers in the spring on the border between Alaska and Canada and in other parts of the gold country.

The letters state that there is a large force of Canadian troops there who are driving all the bad characters to the American side, and if any decent kind of law and order is to be kept when navigation opens, American soldiers must be sent at once. The writers also state that nobody should come into the country without food to last six months or a year.[1]

Washington, D.C., February 11, 1898

At the request of Secretary of War Alger, I called on him at his residence yesterday afternoon, accompanied by Acting Secretary of War Meiklejohn. General Alger has been indisposed for some

---

[1] The first portion of this paragraph is an excellent example of the editorial license various reporters took when reporting on events from the frozen North. In this instance, Wells obviously refused to divulge any but the most vague details of the contents of his letters, so the reporter in question merely filled in what he assumed Wells's mission was about, truth be damned.

weeks past and had returned to bed when we called at four o'clock. We were, however, accorded an interview in his room.

Alger questioned me at length on the Alaskan situation, affairs at Dawson, condition of trail in winter, possibility of getting supplies to Dawson City by Dalton Trail by using reindeer, etc. I informed the Secretary that supplies were badly needed at Dawson, that the use of reindeer was practicable and that there was plenty of moss for them to graze on.

I recommended the Dalton Trail for reindeer and Skagway or White Pass Trail for horses with sleds. In reply to his question concerning the Tanana River, I stated that a big exodus of miners was certain to occur from Klondike to Tanana within six months. There are no supplies on the Tanana at present.

By request of the Secretary of War, I am preparing a detailed report of affairs in Yukon and Alaska, to be used by the Department as it sees fit, in conjunction with Captain Ray's information.

It should be mentioned that I had no intention of leaving Dawson this winter, but Captain Ray's dispatches and letters from Fort Yukon revealed such a grave state of affairs that it became necessary to communicate with the War Department at once. Captain Healy, as Captain Ray's agent at Dawson, asked me to undertake the mission and on three days' notice I was ready for the 700-mile journey through the snow.

A blizzard caught me at Pelly River, 180 miles from Dawson, and destroyed the winter trail on the Yukon. With my three companions I broke a new trail and floundered through heavy snow 450 miles to the coast, carrying the dispatches and accumulating personal data for the use of the Department. This is the story in brief.

Alaska—1897; Up and Down the Yukon[2]

I will begin my story by saying by way of introduction that in December 1897, Captain Ray was isolated at Fort Yukon, Yukon Valley, Alaska. He had with him but one officer, Lieutenant Richardson, and no soldiers at his command. He was in a critical position owing to the turbulent acts of a mob which he was endeavoring to control. In this condition of things he took the opportunity of sending special dispatches from Fort Yukon to Dawson by a Mr. Gasch, who was connected with the North American Trading and Transportation Company. Captain Ray was apparently in the dark, as the mail facilities from Dawson to the United States at that time were not perfect. It was because of this condition of things that he gave the dispatches to Mr. Gasch to hand to one Captain John J. Healy, who was the general manager of the company hitherto referred to. This gentleman resided at Dawson, and was instructed to see that the dispatches named were promptly forwarded to Washington. Mr. Gasch arrived in Dawson about December 15, after most of the winter travelers to the coast had departed. Accompanying Captain Ray's dispatches to the Department was an open letter to Captain Healy, which described the serious state of affairs at Fort Yukon and indicated further trouble. From this letter Captain Healy learned for the first time that there was only 300 tons of provisions at Fort Yukon, belonging to the two trading companies, instead of 1000 tons as he had supposed. The fact was also stated that 800 people were in sight when the dispatches were written.

Captain Healy was very much disturbed over the contents of Captain Ray's open letter. It was known that large numbers of men

[2]This is the complete report Wells wrote for the War Department and submitted to Congress. It is taken verbatim from the U.S. government publication "A Compilation of Narratives of Explorations in Alaska," published in 1900 as ordered by the U.S. Senate.

had proceeded on down the Yukon in skiffs late in the fall, and it appeared quite likely that many of them had arrived at Fort Yukon after Captain Ray's dispatches were written. It seemed that there was a strong probability of very serious complications arising at Fort Yukon, concerning which the Government should have information as early as possible. There was no mail service out of Dawson, and the whereabouts of the United States mail carrier from Circle City to Juneau were unknown. It was generally reported that he had thrown up his contract.

Captain Healy, appreciating the responsibility placed upon him, after some deliberation made a proposition to me. I was, at the date above mentioned, a prospector, miner and a correspondent of a newspaper syndicate. The proposition was to the effect that the North American Transportation and Trading Company would advance $1000 in the name of the Government to pay my expenses in carrying out the dispatches of Captain Ray, and that the Government would settle with me for my services in undertaking this mission. Captain Healy further stated that he was strongly opposed to placing the dispatches in the hands of any man leaving Dawson who was unaccustomed to winter traveling, fearing that some mishap might occur which would prevent the papers from reaching their destination. There was a general belief in Dawson, which was shared by Captain Healy, that the winter trail out to Juneau would be extremely difficult to traverse, and that numbers of men would die of starvation along the route when their insufficient supplies of provisions gave out. More or less trouble was, therefore, anticipated for travelers who were not well provided with food. It was not known that the Canadian Mounted Police were providing food for their needs at various points along the route. Captain Healy was very anxious to have the dispatches placed in as safe hands as possible, and he stipulated with me that, in case I accepted the mission, I should be extremely careful in the selection of the men who were to accompany me.

I accepted Captain Healy's proposition, and, after consuming three days in getting my affairs into shape, selected John Bigelow

200

and Charles Christiansen to accompany me on the trip. Each assistant furnished two dogs. Another man, Charles Lake, also undertook to accompany the party, paying all his own bills and expenses.

On the 20th day of December I left Dawson, accompanied by the men whom I have already mentioned. We had six dogs, provisions, etc., the latter being transported upon two 8-foot sleds, three dogs harnessed to each sled. The winter trail was good almost to Pelly River, which we reached on December 29, the thermometer that evening standing at 40 degrees below zero. During the night there was a rise in temperature of a most phenomenal nature, the mercury jumping to 30 degrees above zero by morning—a change of 70 degrees. The rise in temperature was accompanied by a violent wind storm, which completely destroyed the trail on the river. As no parties of travelers had preceded us for some days, the unpleasant duty devolved upon us of breaking a new trail, which was difficult, owing to the crusty condition of the snow, which would not sustain our weight or that of the sleds. In most places the snow averaged about a foot or 15 inches in depth; also drifts were frequent and the ice was very rough. Coming from Dawson to Pelly River we had averaged nearly 20 miles per day, but with a bad trail, or no trail at all, we were now compelled to force our way at a slower speed; the traveling became very difficult and as we approached the coast frequent winds destroyed the tracks made by preceding dog teams. It was necessary to walk the entire distance from Dawson to the sea coast, which, following the winding of the trail, cannot be less than 650 or 700 miles. The bodily exertion caused by breaking trail and also tramping through heavy snow was necessarily severe. We walked from early morning until late in the evening for thirty-four days, allowing only one day for rest, reaching the sea coast over the Skagway or White Pass on the evening of January 24. The trip across the summit was made through a storm of snow and sleet. On the morning of January 25 I sailed from Skagway for Seattle on the steamship *Rosalie*. The other men remained at Skagway for the time being. They knew nothing of the character of my mission while coming out, or that I carried any dispatches.

Arriving at Seattle on the evening of January 30, I telegraphed at once to the War Department, announcing my arrival and received telegraphic instructions from the Acting Secretary of War, directing me to turn the dispatches over to General Merriam, commanding the Department of Columbia. These instructions were carried out when I delivered the dispatches on the following day to General Merriam at Vancouver Barracks. The trip had been a very arduous one, and I had sacrificed considerable money to make it, as already stated. It seemed to me, therefore, that the amount asked for, viz. $1500, was by no means excessive. Had I made the trip for any private business purpose, in the interest of other individuals, my bill would probably have been somewhat larger. Few men left Dawson this winter who did not expect to make $2000 or $3000. Only a few weeks before Captain Ray's dispatches arrived at Dawson City, Captain Healy had paid an outgoing traveler, who had mining claims to sell in the States, $500 to carry a business letter to Chicago. I have been particular in mentioning these instances so that the situation might be clearly understood.

General Merriam approved both of the bills presented by the transportation company mentioned and myself, and ordered vouchers issued by Quartermaster Jacobs for the payment of the same. I received my personal voucher for $1500, and cashed it at the First National Bank in Seattle, receiving a draft on New York payable to myself. The next morning General Merriam stated to me that some doubt had arisen in his mind as to his authority to pay the bills without first submitting them to the War Department, and asked me to return the voucher pending action by the Department. As I had already cashed the voucher, I handed him the draft which I had received, endorsing it over to Paymaster Jacobs. The voucher for $1000, intended for the transportation company, had been all of the time in the hands of Paymaster Jacobs, he having received from me a receipt for both vouchers, amounting to $2500. The quartermaster handed me a paper addressed to P. B. Weare & Co.,

202

Chicago, notifying them that he held a $1000 draft subject to their orders. This paper is now in the possession of Mr. P. B. Weare.

The expenses which I incurred in making the trip out of Dawson to Seattle amounted to something over $1300, and from Seattle to Washington, D.C., including hotel bills, $120 more, the extra $420 having been paid by me out of my personal funds. It has been my intention to ask the North American Transportation and Trading Company to settle the extra account, inasmuch as I brought them some letters from Captain Healy. I did not bring out any mining claims for sale, nor do I expect to receive money from any source except from the Government and the Weare people, as already stated, in payment for the trip.

During the summer of 1889 I first entered Alaska as the representative of a league of newspapers, and made a journey from Dyea down the Yukon to St. Michael. A few gold miners were at work at that time upon the Forty Mile Creek. In the spring of 1890 I again entered Alaska, this time by way of Chilkat Pass, having made a joint arrangement with a popular illustrated weekly and the United States Coast and Geodetic Survey Office to write descriptive articles and do some geographical work. The Coast Survey furnished scientific instruments, and also free transportation on the United States vessel *Patterson* sailing from San Francisco. While on this expedition, accompanied by four other men, including Jack Dalton, I first gained an insight into the possibility for building a road over what subsequently became the Dalton Trail. No white man had ever before crossed by way of Chilkat Pass. We followed the Indian trail to the headwaters of the Talkeetna, discovering and mapping Lakes Maude and Arkell, and later on mapping the Talkeetna River down to its junction with the Yukon. Subsequently, with three men, including an Indian, I ascended Forty Mile Creek, Lake Mansfield, Razorback Divide, the Toke River and other points on the way. Lack of food then compelled a return to the Tanana, which I descended for some 600 miles to its junction with the Yukon.

In 1897 I again entered the Yukon country, for the third time, choosing the Skagway or White Pass, and reached Dawson on September 20. As a result of observations made on these various trips, I respectfully submit the following statement bearing upon past, present and future conditions in the mining regions of Alaska and of the Northwest Territory: There are undoubtedly large deposits of gold in Alaska, rivaling those of the British Northwest Territory. I noticed excellent mineral indications upon the Tanana River and in other locations in 1890. I discovered a true fissure vein of quartz 8 feet in diameter, with well-defined casing rocks, upon the upper Tanana. This quartz evidently contained metal, specimens of which I secured to take out to San Francisco for assay, but which were subsequently lost in a river catastrophe. Numerous creeks entering the upper Tanana bear colors of gold in the sand. All of the gold-bearing streams of Alaska so far discovered, viz., Birch Creek, Miller Creek, Forty Mile Creek, Sixty Mile Creek, and Seventy Mile Creek, head in the vicinity of the Tanana River and flow away to the northeast. On the southwestern slope and heading near the Tanana are the noted Copper and Susitna rivers, the latter being the gold-bearing stream which has recently come into prominence through the placer discoveries on Cook Inlet. The Copper River is popularly supposed to be located in the heart of a mineral belt. It is a reasonable deduction that if all of the streams flowing away from the upper Tanana on the northeast and the southwest bear gold, that the Tanana itself must cut through a gold-bearing country. This opinion is shared by nearly all of the old-time miners now located at Dawson. Recently excellent prospects were discovered upon American Creek, a tributary of the Yukon in Alaska, just below Forty Mile Creek. The Forty Mile diggings have been well worked out, but Miller Creek, Birch Creek and other streams within the boundaries of Alaska in the Yukon Valley still offer inducements to placer miners.

I do not believe that any better mining region will be discovered in Alaska than will be found in the great Tanana Valley. To the westward of the Tanana rise gigantic chains of mountains, which will make prospecting toward the Kuskokwim and Susitna rivers extremely difficult. From a good point of vantage upon a high mountain near the head of the Copper River I obtained a bird's-eye view of the country to the westward, and beheld the titanic masses of rock upheaved in much the same fashion as the Andes in South America. A range of very tall mountains parallels the Tanana on its westward side, joining at an acute angle with the high Alaskan Range, which sweeps across from the Tanana near Robertson River to the mouth of the Susitna and beyond. To the westward of this V-shaped arrangement of the mountain chain lies the vast unexplored territory of the Kuskokwim. I have ascended the Kuskokwim 800 miles from the sea coast, and found it a broad, deep and somewhat sluggish stream, flowing in from the unknown east. Indian reports state that the Kuskokwim heads up within a three days' overland march of the lower Tanana. A pass is reported to exist by which it can be reached from the lower Tanana. My observations on the lower Kuskokwim do not induce the belief that it came out from a gold-bearing region, but is possible, nevertheless, as its sluggish current would hardly carry colors very far downstream.

Considerable quantities of white moss and lichens are to be found along the Dalton Trail entering the country by way of Chilkat River. It is my opinion that reindeer can be taken over the Dalton Trail with supplies of food for the miners and that the animals will find sufficient food along the route to keep them in good condition. Considerable quantities of willow grow along the creek bottoms and lowlands bordering upon the Yukon. The young willow shoots form a favorite food for the moose which inhabit that region, and it is quite probable that the reindeer would find subsistence upon such food, even were there no lichens and other mosses in the country. I believe that the reindeer can be advantageously used, especially as the snow is not deep, seldom being more than 18 inches in any part of the interior away from the coast. The deer can no doubt dig down through such a shallow covering and find food, as they are obliged to do in their native country. There are considerable areas of grasslands along the Yukon, following the Dalton Trail, and also farther down, at Pelly River and Stewart River. Grass flats of considerable size are to be found along the Tanana and upper Forty Mile Creek. This grass has been successfully used in Dawson and at other points within the past twelve months as forage for horses, and they seem to do well upon it. There are undoubtedly many points along the Yukon and Tanana rivers where sufficient hay can be secured every summer to keep cattle and horses over winter.

It is believed by well-informed men in Dawson that between 30 and 40 tons of gold will be taken out of the Klondike placers during the present winter. Most of this gold will be shipped to the United States upon the river and ocean steamboats next summer, and will prove an allurement, and thousands of people will leave their homes in the States and start for the gold regions.

Major J. M. Walsh, who is in command of the Canadian police upon the Yukon, and who is the highest official of the Dominion in that region, having supreme executive power, informed me that he proposed to rigidly enforce a regulation prohibiting any American or Canadian miner from entering the Klondike district who could not show 1000 pounds of provisions in his outfit when passing the customs officers at Tagish House. He stated his willingness to bond American miners' outfits through British territory to Circle City or other points in Alaska. He also expressed the wish that the American Government would cooperate in enforcing a regulation which would bar any prospector or miner out of Alaska, as well as the British Northwest Territory, who did not carry a year's provisions as part of his outfit.

The Canadian police, by Major Walsh's orders, were supplying winter travelers upon the Yukon with provisions in cases where the same were needed, and refusing to accept payment for the same. Major Walsh informed me that he had given away thousands of pounds of food this winter to people around the upper Yukon. This food he purchased from miners and others, for prices varying from $1.50 to $2 per pound.

There is a well-defined movement in Dawson among pioneer

miners looking to a stampede across the hills to the Tanana in Alaska, 200 miles distant. Much dissatisfaction exists in Dawson over the Canadian mining regulations, and there is a freely expressed feeling against royalties, the cutting down of the size of claims, etc. This feeling is giving a decided impetus to plans looking toward a migration across into Alaska, where the mining laws are more liberal. There appears to be a striking uniformity of opinion among these men regarding the probability of finding gold deposits upon the Tanana. A few men have recently been prospecting over there, and have brought back remarkable reports to others upon the Klondike. I feel certain that before next summer has passed away hundreds of men, if not thousands, will be upon the Tanana. It is a river which can be easily reached from the Yukon from above or below Dawson by following up Sixty Mile Creek or Forty Mile Creek to the Tanana Divide, otherwise known as the Razorback. This ridge, which is easily ascended from the Yukon Valley, is not over 2500 feet in height, according to observations with a boiling-point thermometer. It is always possible to strike a good summer trail across the hills from Dawson to the headwaters of the Tanana without following either of the streams mentioned. The country is rolling, but not mountainous.

As yet there are no trading posts upon the Tanana, and in case of a large invasion of miners into that valley serious trouble is likely to arise over the question of supplies. I am informed that several trading companies propose to send boats up the Tanana next spring to the limit of navigation, hoping to reach a point nearly opposite Forty Mile Creek. There is doubt as to the navigability of the upper Tanana. Lieutenant Allen, who was the first explorer upon the stream, descending it in 1885, states that he believes the limit of navigation is in the vicinity of Bates Rapids, about midway between the source and mouth of the river. In 1890 I descended the Tanana, making a rough survey of the stream, and it is my impression that steamboats can ascend the Tanana almost to its head. There was a good stage of water when I floated down the river, whereas it is quite probable that Lieutenant Allen struck it at a time when the water was comparatively low. As no surveys have since been made upon the stream, it is largely a matter of speculation as to what can be done with steamboats plying upon it.

Malemute dogs are becoming very scarce along the Yukon, and are in great demand for winter sledging. Two winters ago many of the dogs died from the effects of an epidemic. At present good dogs of the native breed sell rapidly along the Yukon in the vicinity of Dawson at prices ranging from $250 to $400 each. These dogs are far superior for draft purposes in winter to Newfoundland or St. Bernard dogs. Experience has demonstrated that these outside dogs soon become footsore when traveling in winter. They cannot stand prolonged exertion, being far surpassed in this respect by the Malemute or Indian dog. At present it costs about $3 per day to support a dog in Dawson, owing to the fact that salmon and other suitable foodstuffs cost $1 per pound.

There were more than a dozen cases of scurvy, well defined, in Dawson before I left there on December 20. Dr. Chambers, one of the most experienced physicians in the place, told me that he expected several hundred cases of the disease and possibly many more would develop in camp before next spring. The disease takes on a severe form in the Yukon country, a number of old miners having died from its effects at Forty Mile Creek in past years. Dr. Chambers attributed the disease to improper diet, or rather the lack of sufficient variety in food. It is possible that there is a sufficient supply of bacon and beans in Dawson to avert any cases of actual starvation until next spring. But it goes without saying that in case other foodstuffs can be secured or imported by way of the upper river the condition of the miners will be very much better and the progress of scurvy checked.

It is my opinion that the food supply of Dawson is inadequate to meet the demands of the population until the middle of next July, when the first steamboats arrive. The condition of affairs is made worse at Dawson by reason of the fact that no provisions can be secured this winter from Fort Yukon, owing to the scarcity of supplies at that point, and it would seem that every pound of provisions which can be taken into Dawson this winter, either by Government expeditions or by private enterprise, would be acceptable. If the present outlook does not mislead, there will be 10,000 people entering Alaska and the British Northwest Territory within the next six months, and famine conditions will become more accentuated.

The possibility of taking supplies through to Dawson from the Pacific Coast depends largely upon the condition of the trail. If Dalton's route over the hills be followed, the stretch of open water along the Yukon between Lake Laberge and the Hootalinqua, some 30 miles, will be avoided. If the relief expedition, however, proceeds over the upper Yukon lakes it will encounter the difficulty of getting around this open water. When I came out a few weeks ago it was found possible to make a detour of the hills for a portion of the distance, and I believe that a military road could be easily cut through the entire distance back from the river, as the hills are not precipitous, nor is the forest growth extremely heavy. The task might require several weeks' time, but the result would be a permanent benefit, as the open water mentioned causes trouble every winter to travelers, and a road constructed around through the hills would be of permanent value.

The Skagway trail is in fine condition this winter. I came across it in a day and a quarter with dogs and sledges, the last day's run being 32 miles. Hundreds of people were on the trail, moving backward and forward. As I descended from the summit toward Skagway the throng of people rapidly increased in numbers. From appearances there were nearly 10,000 people in Skagway and the immediate vicinity, the majority of whom were moving or preparing freight up over the Skagway trail. A report from Dyea indicated trouble on that pass, a snow slide having temporarily stopped all traffic. The Canadian police were portaging considerable quantities of provisions over the Skagway trail, using horses and large sledges. I believe that the Skagway route is better in winter than the Dyea or Chilkoot route to the Yukon.

The temperature in the Yukon Valley during the present winter is above the average. Only once for a few hours did the thermometer drop to 60 degrees below zero at Dawson. Colder weather was experienced on the upper Yukon in early December than was noted in January. While coming out I noticed considerable open water in places along the river. At some points the ice was thin and detours had to be made. My observations, using the thermometer during the early part of my trip out from Dawson, indicated an average of 18 degrees below zero. At Pelly River an Indian broke the thermometer, and further observations could not be made, but it is my belief that at no time during the following days of January did the temperature fall to more than 20 degrees below zero.

There is a plentiful supply of timber along the Klondike and at Dawson. It is not an open, treeless locality, as has been frequently stated. Heavy spruce forests are found upon the lower Klondike, the trees in many instances being 12 and 15 inches in diameter. There is plenty of timber, both green and dried, along the Yukon, from its headwaters to Fort Yukon. The forest growth is also heavy in the Tanana Valley, although the trees will not average more than 10 or 12 inches in diameter. Fairly good lumber can be produced. The growth is mostly northern spruce, with some birch and willow interspersed.

Considerable fresh meat was taken into Dawson by various individuals last fall. Beef cattle were driven in over the Dalton Trail, slaughtered at Pelly River, and the meat rafted down to the Klondike. Several hundred head of sheep were also brought through to the camp. Two rafts loaded with beef were stranded some distance above Dawson, but most of the meat has been sold, not more than 10 or 12 beeves remaining at either point. Numbers of caribou were slaughtered upon the upper Klondike early in the winter, when a large herd of the animals passed on their annual migration. Some 40 moose were also killed in the same vicinity. There is at present little or no meat upon the Yukon above Big Salmon River.

BILLICK, THE ESQUIMAU DOG.

Artist's drawing of Billick, Wells's sled dog, which accompanied an article on E. H. Wells in the February 12, 1898, New York World.

Washington, D.C., February 10, 1898 (Washington Post)

Billick, the Eskimo dog of Mr. E. Hazard Wells, the writer and Alaskan explorer, was visited by many people at the Shoreham yesterday. He pulled 300 pounds of baggage from Dawson City across the country to the coast, making about eighteen miles a day in weather 50 degrees below zero.[3] Billick is a handsome fellow, very broad-chested, iron gray in color, shaggy, and his bushy tail showing clearly the heavy strain of wolf blood in his make-up. He is as kind as any of our domestic dogs to men, but will fiercely attack any strange canine he meets. Regarding him Mr. Wells said:

"Like all Eskimo dogs, he is one-half wolf, which gives him his tremendous strength and qualities of endurance. He will not fare so well here in Washington because the weather is too warm for him. On the trail he can't be coaxed into a tent to sleep, but curls himself up in the snow. Often in the morning I have only been able to tell where he was by a little white mound, the falling snow having covered him up completely in the night and acting as a blanket. The moment I called him he'd jump out of his bed, shake himself, and frisk about as gayly as though he had enjoyed the most luxurious sleeping quarters.

"He cost me $300, which is the average price of his class of dogs at Dawson. Common curs cost $200. The Eskimo are not only scarce, but are more valuable for drawing sleds by virtue of training and inherited qualities. On the trail Billick will eat three pounds of meat a day, which he greatly prefers cooked, but will dispatch raw. Since he has reached civilization, however, he won't touch any kind of raw meat."

Washington, D.C., February 19, 1898

Ananias, with a 100-pound pack of sulphuretted lies upon his back, has tramped out from the Klondike. He is now busily engaged in handing around big nuggets of misinformation to various American newspaper editors.

There is not much truth in the stories of assassination and plun-

---

[3]Another case of exaggeration, as the weather averaged about 20 below zero and Billick had help from the other dogs in the teams.

der. In one or two isolated cases men are known to have been robbed, but not killed. Coming out from Dawson over the ice I had ample opportunity to investigate stories of murder and theft which had been circulated in Dawson, and was unable to substantiate any of them. Some irresponsible person had asserted in Dawson that the noted frontiersman, Jack Dalton, had quarreled with two men at Five Finger Rapids upon the Yukon. It was stated that Jack was shot through the body, and, while dying, had drawn his gun and killed both of his assailants.

The disciple of Ananias who made these statements further avowed that he had himself assisted in lowering the body of Jack Dalton into his grave. Naturally the story caused a great sensation in Dawson. When I reached Five Finger Rapids, coming out last month, I could find no traces of Dalton's grave. When I reached Portland, General Merriam informed me that Jack had been there to see him in the flesh only a few days previously, and was enjoying remarkably good health for a dead man.

At present most of the tough characters are at Fort Yukon, making trouble for Captain Ray. Conditions are bad enough in the Yukon Valley without adding imaginary troubles.

Tramping around on snowshoes amid thousands of little stars is one of the mid-winter privileges of Klondikers. This of itself may seem to be somewhat of a Utopian statement, but it is true, nevertheless. The snowflakes of the Yukon take on the crystalline formation familiarly known as the six-cornered star. I have carefully examined the flakes on the Yukon this winter and found the stars of almost uniform size and shape.

When returning from Alaska in 1891, I had occasion to stop over in the big city on Lake Michigan. A reporter for one of the morning dailies—the *Times,* I believe—asked me for a story for his paper. I gave him one; but it evidently lacked the vinegar which the Chicagoese enjoy with their morning pancakes. So the reporter proceeded to write a story to suit the case. An alleged interview appeared, about one and a half columns in length, and paraded upon the front page, in which I described the murder of some 19

Alaskan Indians, whom I had slain at various points, in a very neat and skillful manner. The bloody details were worked out with astonishing minuteness. One poor fellow, I remember, I killed with a huge club. I have forgotten how the others met their death. Of course, it was a good story, from a Chicago standpoint, and the reporter took the trouble to send me 12 copies of his enterprising journal.

Carry a filter when you go to the Klondike, but leave your smokeless rifle at home. A small filter is very useful in purifying the impregnated waters of the northwestern rivers. Serious disorders are caused by drinking the water in its unfiltered state. Boiling the fluid improves it, but filtering puts on the finishing touches. The water of the Yukon is bad to drink. Never cease to keep that fact in mind. As for your smokeless .30-30 rifles, what good are they in a country where the mid-winter cold freezes up your ammunition so that it will not explode, and the moose stand and laugh at you?

A pie baker who charges $1.50 per pie is one of the rising capitalists of the Klondike. This pie baker is a bald-headed man, whose name I do not now recall, but I do know that he is making a financial success of himself. In his little cabin upon the main street in Dawson he is turning out dried-apple pies as fast as he can fabricate them, and finds it difficult to supply the trade. At the present price of provisions in Dawson the ingredients of a pie cost about 50 cents, so that he makes an even $1 upon every one of the round disks of pastry.

Speaking of pies reminds me of the restaurants in Dawson. Two of them are in operation. The charge per meal is $3.50, or $10.50 per day, and the menu consists of pork and beans, dried apples boiled, bread, pie and coffee. It does not do to turn one's nose up at the price of a Dawson meal, even if one feels that the variety of dishes is somewhat limited.

Brussels carpet costs $4 a yard upon the Klondike. Some people have supposed that there was no such thing as carpeting in the cabins there, but they are mistaken. Quite a number of women have covered the floors of their log dwellings with gayly patterned

214

Brussels, and many of them have cheesecloth lace curtains. Door-knobs are scarce, but two or three people who belong to the smart set have white porcelain knobs upon their unpainted pine doors.

Axes are worth $7 apiece, and are hard to obtain.

There are no more socks in the town. I was one of the fortunate men who got in on the last distribution.

The only handkerchiefs are silk ones, which by some strange freak were imported instead of serviceable linen ones.

Pins are also in demand, being a scarcer article than nuggets. These hints will show you what you ought to take when you go to the Klondike.[4]

Cincinnati, February 24, 1898

Ice at $1 per pound in Dawson!

Incredible as it may appear, ice did reach this lofty price during last June and July. Nobody in the new city on the Klondike had figured upon the necessity for a mid-summer ice supply, if we except one man named Collins, who had cut a small quantity for his own use. When the hot days of June arrived a number of the saloonists in Dawson found the Klondike water altogether too warm for thinning their whiskey, without the addition of ice, and consequently they began an eager search for the much-needed article.

Then the discovery was made that Collins had a corner on the visible ice supply, although no one had attempted to corner it during the preceding winter. The proprietor of the ice was no fool. He recognized his advantage in an instant, and promptly informed his would-be patrons that Klondike ice was worth $1 per pound.

The saloonists squirmed and declared that Collins was attempt-

---

[4]After completing his business with the War Department in Washington, D.C., Wells returned to Cincinnati, where the following articles were written, concluding the story of his trip.

ing robbery, but all to no purpose. No ice could be obtained unless the price was forthcoming. In the end the saloon men bought the ice and Collins got the gold dust, a neat sum by the way.

During the present winter two men are cutting ice for the purposes of sale next summer; but, judging from the small quantity harvested up to the middle of December, I suspect that the two gentlemen have formed a sort of ice trust between themselves, and that prices are to be maintained next summer.

The saloonists and others who got bit seem to be blissfully unconscious of the scheme, having, in the rush of events, forgotten all about the ice famine of 1897.

I do not mean to advise anyone to take their ice along with them when going to the Klondike this year, but would suggest that freezers for ice cream be left behind.

Word comes to me from a small town near Peoria, Illinois, that a company of Klondikers are preparing for speedy departure, choosing the Copper River route. These men intend to take a piano along. One of their number is a musician, and they have a thrifty idea that in case no gold deposit is found they can give concerts in the mining camps and reap a big harvest.

Now, the concert idea is all right, but the piano idea is all wrong. No human contrivance, short of a balloon, could elevate a piano over the summit of the Copper River range. If the airship should be pressed into service I fear the piano would have its legs scratched when descending into the spruce forests beyond the mountains. It is not advisable to go Klondiking with a piano.

The Dawson burial ground, located on the side of a hill just back of town, had three mounds last December to mark the spot. There was no fence nor gravestones, and the graves were placed in spaces between the forest trees. It is a lonesome spot, the snow-shrouded spruces giving it an indescribably dreary appearance.

In summer the wild flowers bloom in great profusion on the hillside, and can be used for floral decorations, but in winter the mourners at a funeral contribute artificial flowers to decorate the coffin.

216

The trading companies do not bring coffins to Dawson, but import the metal trimmings, handles, etc., and the local carpenters furnish the boxes. Naturally, people do not care to depart from this terrestrial sphere while intent upon accumulating a store of the metal which paves the Celestial City, but I very much fear that ere another December rides down upon the storms, the Death Angel will claim many more victims whose last resting place will be the Dawson Cemetery.

Bearded men are seldom encountered upon the Yukon, the climate being unfavorable for the development of luxuriant whiskers. The reason is a simple one. During the winter the moisture of the breath freezes upon any hair on the upper or lower lip, soon forming a long pendant icicle, sometimes six inches in length. This is no exaggeration. I speak from experimental knowledge.

It does not take men long to find out the fact after reaching the Yukon and the shaving mug and razor are called into use. A supply of razors have been imported into Dawson and sold at $4 each. Strops cost $2.50 apiece. I mention these facts because so many writers in the States like to dilate upon the ferocious appearance of the bearded men of Alaska.

The picture papers often make the beards a foot long. Yukoneers may be a desperate set of men, but we believe in a clean shave.

Billick, my Eskimo dog, has developed a strong dislike to civilized dogs and thrashes them whenever he has an opportunity. The other day he escaped into the street and within three minutes had chastised two dogs and dispatched one chicken. Billick has not met a bulldog yet, and it may be best for the Eskimo to let such alone. He can well afford to rest content with dining on Newfoundlands, spitz dogs and the like.

Billick does not understand the theory of the glass window. In the Eskimo village from which he came glass peekholes are not fashionable, and doors are usually wide open, at least in the summertime.

Billick has sized up the large glass windows about Cincinnati as so many doors, and he has on several occasions tried to go through them when in a hurry. I fear that it will take a long and arduous training to adapt him to the ways of this country.

Cincinnati, February 25, 1898

Billick, the magnificent Eskimo dog brought out from the Klondike by E. Hazard Wells, the *Post*'s Alaskan explorer, is attracting much attention in Cincinnati, having appeared several times upon the streets. Billick wears a heavy mastiff's collar, to which is attached a strong chain, at which he tugs with surprising power.

In Washington last Saturday afternoon, Billick created a scene on F Street. He was out walking with Wells and encountered his first cat. At the sight of the strange creature Billick became transfixed, rooted to the spot for the moment, with ears erect.

Then, with a brief, expressive yelp which seemed to say: "A gray mink, by Jove!" he sprang fiercely to the attack, dragging his master forcibly into the street. The cat took one look at the wolf-like visage of the Klondike canine and then fled in dismay for the nearest alley, Billick pursuing and taking Wells by force across the street. A sharp touch of the whip brought the dog to a halt and the cat escaped.

In Washington, Billick also beheld his first chickens and, taking them for grouse, nearly succeeded in making a meal of one of them before his intention was detected.

The only thing so far which has fazed Billick is a mogul locomotive. One of these monsters whistled at him in Chicago and Billick lowered his tail and decamped in hot haste.

On the way across the continent, from Seattle to Washington, Billick was a center of attraction. On the trains en route hundreds of passengers visited him in the baggage cars and soon dubbed him "gold dog." He appeared to like the attentions paid him.

Many persons were cautious in approaching Billick, fearing that he would bite. His appearance so strongly suggests the wolf that it is little wonder. Yet his dogship is complacent with all men, never offering to molest. He takes delight, however, in terrorizing other dogs, and is said to be able to whip any so-called civilized dog in one round of three minutes.

One noticeable thing about the Eskimo is his enormous bushy tail, which he carries triumphantly aloft. He has a springy step and an air of absolute confidence. Billick is reported to be looking for a bulldog on which to polish his teeth.

Recently he has discarded dried fish as an article of diet and evinces a strong preference for cooked beef. He will not touch bread, potatoes or other food of that sort. His appetite demands three pounds of meat per day. In the Klondike food for Billick would cost $1 per pound, or $3 per day.

Cincinnati, February 28, 1898

Small things occupy a large share of one's attention on the Klondike.

The matter of buttons is a case in point. There are buttons to be had at the stores in Dawson, if you don't care particularly about kinds and colors, but matching is out of the question.

One day I lost a black button off of my Seattle mackintosh coat, and was obliged to accept from the store a black disk of sufficient size to cause an eclipse of the moon.

There is no black linen thread in Dawson, nothing except the white brand, and so the miners are obliged to sew on buttons with white thread, or worse, employ red silk.

Again comes the question of firewood. Good, dry wood sells at $35 per cord delivered, and most of the Dawsonites find it hard to purchase, even at that price. The surrounding hills are covered with timber, but nobody cares to cut wood.

Everybody wants to dig gold. Some people burn green wood, which requires much attention. More than once I have been driven to the verge of desperation by the obstinate refusal of the green wood of the Yukon to warm itself into a cheerful blaze. In the cabin, with its small sheet-iron stove, one has to tend fire all day long to prevent it from going out.

Water is another source of annoyance. Place a pailful of it by the stove during the evening and the next morning the whole is a chunk of ice. Now this wouldn't be so bad were it not for the fact that the Alaska Commercial Company, in its San Francisco wisdom, sent a large cargo of paper pails into this country for use by the miners. How to thaw out the frozen contents of a paper pail is a problem that no one has been able to solve.

Footwear is one other source of mid-winter vexation and trouble. Moccasins you must wear, of course. They are scarce and high-priced at present, especially the sizes that are required by the feet of newcomers. Last summer the trading companies brought in from the lower Yukon a large quantity of moccasins which had been manufactured by the coast Eskimos. These people, taking their own small feet for patterns, had manufactured the footwear accordingly. At Dawson it was discovered that the moccasins could not be used, there being no Cinderellas in town. Hundreds of pairs were discarded for this reason.

The store moccasins which I purchased in Dawson fell short both as regards length overall and extreme breadth amidships. In my dilemma I secured the services of a Yukon squaw who, in consideration of $5 in gold dust paid to her, fabricated a real comfortable pair of moose-skin moccasins.

Subsequently I secured a large pair of seal-skin boots and a second pair of moccasins, being much better fixed for the winter than were the majority of Dawson men. Moccasins soon wear out, yet they are indispensable in cold weather. Leather shoes or boots are never worn. The feet would freeze in them. It is the custom to wear three or four pairs of socks inside of the moccasins, including one pair of heavy Germans.

It would be possible to go on all day illustrating the difficulties of winter life in Dawson, but this one chapter of ills ought to be sufficient. There is really a thankful side to the picture. The Yukon mosquitoes are all asleep in their sprucewood bunks.

The memories of their vindictive attacks during the summers of bygone years spent in Alaska still haunt me, and I find myself wondering how the thousands of newcomers in the Yukon country will stand it when the bloodthirsty wretches become reincarnated and make their first onslaughts in June of '98. The Yukon mosquito has an unpleasant propensity for unprovoked pugnacity, and he labors without ceasing twenty-four hours for his daily blood.

Read Mr. Cotterill's Letter from Chicago in this Number

The Seattle Mail and Herald

A Social and Critical Journal of the Northwest

Volume V. No. 33.   Price Five Cents at All News S

*Photo and half tone made especially
for the Mail and Herald.*

E. HAZARD WELLS.

Editor of the Seattle Daily Star. Mr. Wells came to Seattle from the South three years ago with the avowed intention of establishing "the only daily paper in the United States that dares to print the news." His threat has been fulfilled. He has since become a full fledged Washingtonian. In substantiation of this statement we cite the self-evident fact that he carries an umbrella in June.

Seattle, Washington   June 28, 1902.

E. H. Wells, publisher and "man-about-town" of Seattle, circa 1902.

And so concludes the story of E. Hazard Wells's Alaskan journey. Wells spent the rest of 1898 and most of 1899 touring the East with his wife and daughter, lecturing on the Klondike, enjoying his sudden celebrity. Finally, he and his family moved to Seattle, Washington, where Wells founded the Seattle *Star,* and set in motion the chain of events which resulted in my coming into possession of his writings.

And what of the relief expedition which Wells, Captain Healy, Captain Ray and others had hoped the United States government would send to the Klondike?

In fact, the Congress had begun preparations for that expedition before Wells began his journey from Dawson to Washington, D.C. On December 9, 1897, a resolution was introduced in the U.S. Senate looking to the relief of people in the Klondike gold fields, and on December 16, 1897, a bill for the same purpose was introduced in the House of Representatives, which was passed and became law on December 18, 1897. Of course, because mail and communications between Washington, D.C., and Dawson City was nearly impossible, and took months at best, Wells and the others had no way of knowing that this measure even existed, and so believed that it was up to them to spur the Congress to act.

In its final version, the bill authorized that the sum of $200,000 be appropriated to be expended at the discretion and under the direction of the Secretary of War, for the purchase of subsistence stores, supplies and materials for the relief of people who were in the Yukon River country or any other mining region of Alaska, and to purchase transportation and provide means for the distribution of those supplies. The bill provided that the consent of the Canadian government must first be obtained in order that the Secretary of War might extend the relief provided into Canadian territory.

Finally, the bill authorized the Secretary of War to use the U.S. Army in carrying into effect the provisions of the act. At his discretion he was further authorized to purchase and import reindeer, and employ and bring into the country reindeer drivers, not citizens of the United States, or to provide any other means of transportation for the relief mission as he might deem practicable. When the relief mission was completed, and the Secretary of War could find no further use for the supplies, he was authorized to turn them over to the Department of the Interior and the proceeds arising from all sales of the reindeer were to be recovered into the Treasury.

The Secretary of War subsequently hired Dr. Sheldon Jackson, an officer of the Interior Department, and instructed him to proceed to Norway and Sweden to purchase 500 domestic reindeer, with sleds, harness and drivers, and transport them to the United States.

Dr. Jackson's expedition landed in New York on the steamer *Manitoban* on February 27, 1898, with 118 drivers and their families, 538 head of reindeer, 418 sleds, 411 sets of harness and a large quantity of reindeer moss for forage. After advertisement a contract was made with the Pennsylvania Railroad Company to transport the expedition to Seattle for $10,418.75. The reindeer train arrived in Seattle on March 7, 1898, without accident or loss and with the animals in excellent condition, the run across the continent having been made on time.

Early in January, however, reports had begun to reach the War Department and the Interior Department which suggested that the accounts of destitution and threatened starvation on the Klondike were greatly exaggerated. In fact, as it was subsequently discov-

This Anders Wilse photograph shows the reindeer of the ill-fated relief mission at rest in Woodland Park, in Seattle. The deer were the hit of the city, and hundreds of Seattleites came to see them during their stay. (Photograph courtesy of the Historical Photograph Collection, University of Washington Libraries.)

This Anders Wilse photograph shows some of the reindeer drivers from Lapland hired to help with the relief expedition, sitting with their families on the porch of the place where some of them stayed in Seattle. (Photograph courtesy of the Historical Photograph Collection, University of Washington Libraries.)

ered, the temporary shortages that had occurred during the fall and early winter were primarily caused by miners and other private parties hoarding all the supplies they could get their hands on, hoping to drive up the prices and make a killing by selling their goods at the artificial-panic rates.

By the time the relief expedition reached Seattle on March 7, it was common knowledge that there was not a true shortage, and so the Secretary of War made the decision to cancel the relief expedition.

Rather than declare the effort a total loss, the Secretary decided to turn the relief expedition into three separate reconnaissance missions, with the purpose of ascertaining possible routes of travel to the gold fields of Alaska and the British Northwest, mapping possessions of the United States and furnishing relief to any inhabitants who were found in want and destitution.

The reindeer and drivers were shipped on the steamship *Seminole* from Seattle, on March 16, 1898, and arrived at Haines Mission, Alaska, on March 29.

On April 4, 1898, 326 reindeer, together with their Lapp drivers and their families, were turned over to the jurisdiction of the Interior Department. The other 200 reindeer (12 of the original 538 died between Seattle and Haines Mission) remained the property of the War Department.

The three reconnaissance missions, as it turned out, were as ill-fated as the original relief expedition from which they were derived.

Expedition No. 1, under the command of Captain Bogardus Eldridge, was recalled. It was supposed to go over the Dalton Trail into the Yukon country, but too many of the reindeer died, and, in the words of a Captain Brainerd, "the rest of the creatures were useless for the purpose for which they were procured." It was discovered en route to Haines Mission and thereafter that the reindeer were much more finicky eaters than had been originally assumed, and were not interested in any of the forage provided for them on the voyage to Alaska and after arrival at the Mission. As a result, the animals became extremely sick, and were dying at the rate of twenty a day by early May.

Expeditions Nos. 2 and 3 were stopped by General Thomas Anderson, in command of the Lynn Canal Military District. The reindeer of both expeditions, as with expedition No. 1, had become sick and weak and were useless for any purpose, much less bearing heavy loads over steep inclines. General Anderson had a U.S. government mule packtrain at his disposal, but he refused to let the expeditions substitute his animals for their own failing reindeer. The primary reason for this, as was subsequently revealed, was that the general's military sensibilities were offended by the fact that, since the soldiers leading the expeditions were on a mission for the U.S. Interior Department, and also didn't want to upset their Canadian neighbors, they were compelled to don civilian clothes and carry all the usual accouterments (weapons, decorations, rank designations, etc.) concealed under same. So General Anderson, vehemently opposed to soldiers wearing anything but uniforms, decided not to help expeditions Nos. 2 and 3, and that was the end of them.

What became of the 118 immigrants and their families after their contract with the U.S. government expired is unknown. They were paid a total of $13,559.70 from the time they were hired until their contract ran out on January 31, 1899. After most of the reindeer had perished, and the various missions had been abandoned as failures, it is known that at least some of the immigrants returned to Seattle, where many of their descendants live today. But in the spring of 1898, the world's attention was turned to the Spanish-American War, and so the exact fate of the 118 Lapp drivers and their families remains something of a mystery even to this day.

APPENDIX I

The following is the story of Dr. J. W. Van Sant's experiences in Dawson, written after his return to Peoria, Illinois.

When Phillips and I tied up our boat at Dawson City amid a hundred other boats on the Klondike, it was four o'clock in the afternoon and twilight. We went ashore and took the first convenient spot we could find for pitching our tent. We were welcome to take any unoccupied place.

Dawson is situated on a level where the Yukon and Klondike come together and form a very good site for a town, though high water would reach some of the cabins nearest the stream.

I found a level and set up my Lares and Penates (cook stove, bed, table, etc.) and was ready for the business that had brought me to the Klondike. My next-door neighbor was an entire stranger, and it seems that the choice spirits of the world had come to that far northern habitation, for everybody was kind, helpful and unselfish. My neighbor said that he would keep an eye on my tent and belongings and would see that no dogs got at the food. There was no fear that humans would molest it.

We found ourselves so eager to join in the search for gold that we did not wait to build a cabin, though the winter was coming on. The second or third day after our arrival we started to "rustle"

229

for a claim. The great bulk of the claims were already marked off along Bonanza and El Dorado, so we were obliged to test the soil on the outskirts of these, or hunt new streams.

I gathered together enough edibles to last me two or three days, took an extra tent and struck out. Fearing thieves, I asked the Gold Commissioner what would happen if I should kill a robber. "Shoot him first," he replied, "and then come and see me about it." This gentleman is a good churchman, and leads the singing at the mission.

Four of us started out from Dawson for El Dorado Creek, where we could still find gold land. It was a 30-mile tramp, but, having become used to walking, it was not very hard work. We struck the forks of El Dorado and got our miner's pans. Stooping down, we filled them half full with sand and gravel, then dipped them in the water. I had often panned in other mining camps and could do the trick deftly. The first pan showed me a "color," that is, minute grains of gold in the corner of the pan. I could only guess as to how much it would run to the ton. Of course, unless the quantity was large, it would never pay in a country where living and other expenses are $10 to $15 per day.

But we tried pan after pan, here and there and everywhere, all showing more or less free gold. Then we picked out the most likely strip and measured off 500 feet up and down the fork for each of us four. We made stakes, drove them into the hard ground, wrote our names on the stakes, and the claims were ours, ready to be recorded. We were well satisfied, though of course it was problematical just how much gold we would get out. I know now, however, that I have good ground, and I left it in safe hands to work.

As the law will not permit you to locate more than one claim in one district, we determined to seek farther on. By this I mean new territory drained by streams that do not run into the Klondike or its tributaries.

So we crossed over the divide to Indian Creek, to which point there was a stampede. We panned the earth in certain unclaimed localities there and found color in Quartz or Little Blanche Creek.

The crowd was coming in so fast we had no time to hesitate. I staked off the second claim above Discovery. The divide is a wooded mountain and must be full of gold, though no one could tell just where it is in it. In this Indian Creek district we were allowed to measure off by 200 feet, and every other 200 feet was set apart for the Crown. That diminishes your chances now just one-half all over the British Northwest Territory. Canada doesn't propose to get left.

I asked of everyone I ran across in Dawson if he knew of any comers from Peoria or vicinity. There wasn't a soul I knew. I had met E. Hazard Wells at the lakes coming in, and hunted him up at Dawson. Through him I ran across Frank Harvey Piel. I discovered that Wells belonged to the Yukon Order of Pioneers, and stood in with the all-powerful trading companies. He helped many a poor devil to get a sack of flour who couldn't have got it for love or money. He was always into something. When the church burned he was one of the prime movers to get supplies for the poor fellows who had lost their all. He made a speech in a quiet way and it struck straight home, and all the fellows who had lost their provisions were soon helped to grub and goods again. So well did Wells make his way among the Dawsonites that he didn't have to build a cabin—Bill Liggett, an old pioneer, made him his tenant free in a very nice cabin.

I left Dawson to return to Peoria on November 23, and reached Skagway in twenty-seven days. Piel started off with me, but he was a "Skukum man" and beat me out. A "Skukum" is an all-round good man, in Indian parlance, and Piel deserved the name. I don't know where he got away from me, but there were nine in the party, with sixteen dogs, and we would get three or four miles apart. We were both trying to make fast time.

The 650 miles of journey was anything but an easy march. One of my party, a banker, gave out, and had to stop at a cabin, where he prepared to lodge until spring. We got in straits once, parted with some of our grub, and I gave a man $62 for a sack of flour. This news went ahead, somehow, and when I came out I found that

231

the Associated Press had reported me in destitute circumstances. I had given a man a letter, but he fell into the river and wet the writing, so he couldn't make out the meaning or the address. So he scattered the news broadcast from Seattle, hoping the right party would hear of it and come to my relief. But I really didn't get into dire distress at all, and the report only unnecessarily alarmed my relatives and friends. But some did suffer greatly trying to get out. I saw a boy lying in a hut with both feet frozen black. He expected to die there.[1]

Most of our party got on famously. Our dogs were of the best, and I gave $200 to $300 apiece for them. The sleds were loaded as light as possible. We carried almost nothing but our food, bedding, stove and tents.

We started out on the river ice and went in whatever line was smoothest. The snow was two feet deep most of the 650 miles, but it was packed down, and, as long as we stayed on the trail, it was all right. But if we got off we were up to our waists in the light snow. The thermometer registered 30 degrees below zero most of the way.

We passed from one to five dog teams every day. If we got started early we would come on a lighted tent, where the inmates were getting breakfast. We would hurry on. At one place the country was so mountainous we had to hoist the sleds up a cliff 200 feet high, and at another place we lifted them 75 feet. At the swift Whitehorse Rapids the river was not frozen, and we, of course, had to take to the banks. There was 30 miles of open river, and frequently we sledded along the shore ice.

Sometimes we would find ourselves in a corner and we would lose much time in retracing our steps. I wore my "muck-lucks," or skin boots, and jeans overalls, and tramped on foot the whole 650 miles, nearly as far as from Cincinnati to New York. Unless a

---

[1]Probably William Byrne, of Chicago, prior to the time the doctor amputated both his feet and before Wells's encounter with the boy at the cabin near McCormack's Post.

man can stand walking 20 to 25 miles per day, he ought not attempt that journey.

We passed a number of government police with supplies and often came upon an abandoned camp, which we would utilize for our own purposes for the night. I consider we had a very lucky trip. There were at least 2000 at Dawson who wanted to come out, but feared to undertake the journey.

Well, finally we reached Skagway. From that point home, to Peoria, Illinois, was the ordinary travel.

The trip cost me $2100, 45 pounds of avoirdupois and nearly six months' time. Not one out of a hundred will be as lucky as I was, and I didn't make a fortune, but I have two claims and will go back to work them.

APPENDIX II

The following is a transcription of Wells's handwritten ledger for his Klondike trip up to the point he left Dawson on December 20, 1897. His expenses on the trip out were kept separately and were not anywhere in the collection.

Expenditures—Klondike Trip

Powell & Clements, gum, etc.	$20.15
Messengers	.95
Sleeper	2.00
Excess baggage	.90
Camera & plates	39.00
Rubber blankets (2)	2.50
1 yard of rubber cloth	.75
1 pair rubber boots	5.00
Rubber cement	.10
Tea	1.25
Expressman	1.00
Underwear	3.50
Neckties (2)	.25
Hat	1.50
Socks	.25

Street car	$ .10
Pressing suit	1.60
Bus & bag @ Chicago	1.00
Porter to Chicago	.20
Sleeper to St. Paul	2.00
Breakfast @ Chicago	.25
Street car	.05
Refreshments	.10
Papers	.25
Dinner	.45
Morton Park ticket	.34
Baggage fee, Chicago	.20
Postage	.20
Supper @ Chicago	.45
Checkroom @ Chicago	.20
Six dozen 5 x 7 camera plates	5.10
Camp kit	9.00
Flask	1.00
Waiter (St. Paul)	.30
Whiskey for flask	.75
Bath	.25
Refreshments	.30
Carryall bag, St. Paul	4.00
Pack sack, St. Paul	2.50
Hotel, St. Paul	1.75
Lunch, St. Paul	.25
Sleeper to Seattle (Tourist)	5.00
Mosquito netting	.80
Supper on train	.50
Breakfast on train	.40
Shave on train	.25
Dinner on train	.90
Supper on train	.60
Breakfast on train	.65
Dinner on train	.65

Oranges on train	$ .25
Supper on train	.50
Breakfast on train	.75
Porter on train	.50
Observation car, for writing	.50
Postage stamps	.50
Alaska ticket	40.00
Photo plates	2.20
Stove (½ interest)	4.00
Clothing for Yukon River	14.00
Hardware	8.65
Pack straps	1.50
Provisions (Seattle Grocery)	90.00
Boat (½ interest)	12.50
Hardware	1.10
Stationery	2.50
Veil for gnats	.35
Gloves, one pair (buckskin)	1.25
Hat for Yukon	2.00
Rubber changing sack	1.75
Shoes re-soled	1.00
Supper in Seattle	.45
Telegram to Cincinnati *Post*	1.61
Three granite kettles (½ interest)	1.25
Frying pan (½ interest)	.20
Reflector (½ interest)	.75
Medicines	1.00
Photos of self	.25
Corks	.35
Photo	.50
Dinner	.20
Horses, two (½ interest)	25.00
Packsaddles, two (½ interest)	3.50
Messenger	.25
Street car	.10

Horse feed	$ 4.00
Hauling feed	1.38
Shoeing horse	1.50
Oats	1.05
Freight on oats	.45
Boat porter	.25
Hardware (½ interest)	1.60
Freight on horse to Skagway	22.50
Porter	.25
Telescope valise @ Seattle	4.00
Dinner @ Seattle	.60
Horse blanket	1.50
Pins	.04
Blue shirt	3.00
Necktie	.25
Doctor for prescriptions	1.25
Medicines for Yukon	2.55
Lock	.25
Photo tray	.70
Books	.40
Paper	.05
Stationery	.25
Freight to Skagway	8.20
Supper @ Seattle	.50
Provisions	.50
Freight to Skagway (additional)	4.15
Changing coat back	1.00
Storage of trunk, Ball & Co., Seattle	1.80
Dray	.50
Room @ Seattle (two days)	2.00
Alaska map	1.50
Steward on *Rosalie*	.50
Photo	.50
Sacks at Metlakatla	.45
Rubber shoes at Metlakatla	.60

Shawl at Metlakatla	$ .60
Provisions at Metlakatla	1.00
Meals at Skagway	2.50
Postage at Skagway	.25
Citric acid at Skagway	.25
Meals at Skagway (4)	2.75
Hauling at Skagway	.50
Packing at Skagway	1.00
Meal at Skagway	1.00
Socks at Skagway	.50
Landing horses (2) at Skagway	5.00
Bag	1.00
Wagonload of goods hauled partway to bridge	6.00
Repairs to road toll	1.00
Horse nose-bags (2)	2.50
Provisions	3.00
Packing	1.00
Hauling feed to foothills	1.50
Sacks	1.50
Man at bridge	1.00
Wagon to end of bridge	3.00
Boat at Lake Bennett	90.00
Sail for boat at Lake Bennet	10.00
Nails for boat at Lake Bennet	7.00
Pitch for boat at Lake Bennet	8.00
Beef @ Five Finger Rapids	3.00
Three bear skins	24.00
Granite pail	4.00
Condensed milk	1.00
Dried moose meat	1.50
Fresh cabbage	1.00
Handkerchief	.25
Provisions @ Dawson City	94.45
Letter postage to U.S.	2.00
Provisions	.25

Assistant Gold Commissioner (services)	$10.00
Sacks (2)	1.00
Cap	1.50
Haircut & shave	1.50
Meals @ Dawson Restaurant	1.25
Provisions @ Dawson Restaurant	17.50
Meal at Dawson City	.75
Stove at Dawson City	41.00
Meals at Dawson City	2.25
Gold pan	2.00
Tape line	1.75
Sugar—25 lbs.	7.50
Beef	12.00
Citron melon	1.00
Cream of tartar	.50
Candy	1.00
Mirror	1.00
Tea	2.00
Provisions	33.75
Beef	6.40
Salmon @ 7.00/lb.	4.50
Spruce board	2.88
Nails	.25
To Waller for cutting wood	15.00
Lamp	7.00
Ax	2.00
Crosscut saw	5.00
Pail	1.50
Cake box	1.50
Chamber pot	1.50
Stew pan	1.00
Frying pan	2.50
Netting	4.50
Liggett for flour	6.00
Needles	.25

Expenditures Klondyke trip.

One of the pages of Wells's handwritten ledger.

Thread	$ .25
2 whisk brooms	1.50
Tacks	.25
Heavy blanket shirt	6.50
Moccasins (one pair)	1.50
Drawers (one pair)	2.50
Towels	1.00
Yarn	.50
Darning needle	.25
Timber permit	2.75
Handkerchiefs	1.50
White cloth	.25
Meat	5.00
Bacon	5.00
Candles	2.00
Socks (German)	2.50
Muslin	.25
Provisions	.25
Butter	1.25
Gum	1.00
Flour (store clerk)	6.00
Bacon (12 pounds)	6.00
Conditioning cream	1.50
Butter	2.50
Rolling pin	.75
Shave	.50
Table cover	.50
Ink & pens	.75
Church contribution, Dawson	.50
Beef	3.00
File	.75
Reflector (lamp)	1.00
Suspenders	1.50
Cartridges—20, .45-90	2.00
Pan	.75

Glue & cheesecloth	$ .50
Fixing camera	.50
Mukluk soles	2.00
Lard (replacement of same stolen from me)	4.00
Bacon (53 lbs.)	26.50
Lard (duplicated)	4.00
Maple syrup (1 gallon)	3.00
Case of corn	12.00
Condensed milk (2 doz. cans)	12.00
Salt (5 lbs.)	.50
Haircut and shave	1.50
Razor and strop	6.50
Stick of big wood	5.00
Tablecloth	1.00
Baking powder (4 cans)	2.00
Wire stand for table	.25
Lynx skin for cap	7.00
Cloth for cap	.65
Shirt	6.50
Crosscut saw	6.00
Red flannel (2 yds.)	2.50
Provisions @ Healy's store	9.75
Fur cap	25.00
Table cover	5.00
Calico & muslin	1.75
Handkerchief	2.00
Shirt	6.50
Yukon Order of Pioneers dues	20.00
Mending parkie	1.00
Agate-ware	2.00
Towel	1.00
Church	1.00
White drill	1.20
Moccasins	3.00
Restaurant meal	1.50

Drawers	$ 5.00
Socks	3.00
Gum	.50
Dentistry	15.00
Chimney	.50
Broom	3.00
Ax	7.00
Soap	.50
Coal oil (2 gallons)	3.00
Gum	.50
Haircut	1.00
Tin pail	3.50
Sawing wood	3.00
Provisions	1.00
Provisions	2.50
Flour	25.00
Church	.50
Cloth & canned goods	3.00
Red blanket	22.00
Gum	1.00
Sheepskin	2.00
Thermometer	3.50
Provisions	6.00
Dues in Y.O.O.P. (through October '98)	20.00
Firewood (one cord)	35.00
Total Expenditures—Klondike Trip	$1311.60

INDEX

Aares, Lake, 74
Adams Creek gold claims, 81
Adney, Chappan, 106
Alaska, *passim*: gold fever and
    development of, 6–7 (*see also* Gold;
    specific aspects, places); maps (*see*
    Maps); report by Wells to the United
    States government on conditions of
    gold prospectors in (*see under* Wells,
    E. Hazard); winter in (*see* Winter,
    Arctic). *See also* specific
    developments, places
Alaska Commercial Company, 3–4, 80,
    85, 87, 88, 89, 90, 129, 133, 139, 145,
    151, 152, 157, 160–61, 220
Alaskan Range, 205
Alger, Russell A., 197–98
Allen, Lieutenant, 196, 207
Allen, George, 71
All Gold Creek claims, 81
Alsek River, 193–94, 195
American Creek, 204
Ames, Billy, 31
Anderson, General Thomas, 228
Apples, dried, 52; pies, 214
Arctic nights, beauty of, 93; Aurora
    Borealis, 93, 105
Arctic Press Association, 105–8
Arkell, Lake, 193, 194, 203
Arkell, W. J. (Arkell's expedition), 84,
    192, 193–95
Associated Press, 84
Axes, 112, 215
Ayan Indians, 161. *See also* Indians

Bacon, 30, 48–49, 51, 52, 54–55, 56, 57,
    61, 80, 85, 86, 87, 99–100, 111, 167,
    178, 182, 208
Baking powder, 35, 47, 51, 57, 111, 116,
    167, 181
Barbershops, 139, 159
Bates Rapids, 207
Beans, 35, 45, 48, 52, 57, 61, 80, 85, 87,
    111, 208, 214
Bear (steamer), 194
Bear Creek gold claims, 81
Beards, 217

Bears, 47, 159; silver-tip, 47, 48
Bedoe, Frank, 88
Beef. *See* Meat supplies
Bench claims, 82; size of, 82. *See also*
    Claims, gold
Bennett, Lake, 186
Bering Sea, 3, 83
Bicket, Dr., 179
Bigelow, John, 165, 166, 168, 169–70,
    172–74, 176, 178, 184–85, 187,
    200–1
Big Salmon River, 210; Canadian post at,
    180–81, 192, 196
Billick (sled dog), 165, 166, 188, 211–
    12, 217–19; drawing of, 211; food for,
    cost of, 167, 212, 219
Birch Creek, 142, 204
Biscuits, 57, 167, 172
Blankets, 5, 89, 91, 110, 112, 119, 165,
    166, 168
Blueberries, 47, 48, 64
Boats (watercraft), 14, 15–16, 22, 23,
    29–30, 32, 38, 43–45, 46–47, 53, 68,
    112; building, 29–30, 43–45, 46–47,
    53, 112; canoes, 5, 14; canvas, folding,
    112; cost of, 29–30, 32, 44, 55, 70;
    portaging (*see* Portaging); rafts, 43, 92,
    95, 112, 172; scows, 37; sectional, 14,
    21, 32, 112; skiffs, 23 (*see also* Skiffs);
    steamers (*see* Steamboats)
Boggs, John, 152
Boiler, James, 137
Bolton, E. D., 81, 82
Bonanza Creek, 81, 103, 104, 192; gold
    claims, 81; gold strikes, 192
Boots. *See* Footwear
Boulder Creek gold claims, 81
Brainerd, Captain, 227
Bread, 32, 35, 45, 57, 63, 86, 111, 116,
    214
Breck, Samuel, 195
Bridges (bridge-building), 24, 26, 28
British, the, 41, 74–76; British Columbia,
    10, 11, 35; British Northwest
    Territory, 113, 204, 206, 209, 227,
    231. *See also* Canada; specific places
British Yukon Company, 41

245